Rapid Development with Adobe® Captivate® 5 for Windows

By Daniel Novak, M.A.

with Mary Burkart, M.S.

Copyrights

Rapid Development with Adobe® Captivate® 5 for Windows

Copyright Daniel Novak, 2010.

Written by Daniel Novak, M.A. (http://daniel-novak.com)

with Mary Burkart, M.S.

Dedication

To Mark and Mona Novak for their boundless support, my brothers (my heroes), my teachers, and my friends. Special thanks to Doug Lucas for giving me the opportunity to teach and learn at the Big Q, and all of my coworkers for their input and ideas.

-Daniel Novak, San Diego, 2010

To Russ, thank you for your sacrifice. To Matt, Joel, and Bethany thank you for so generously giving up time with mom for the past year! To Pam Sexton: thanks for sharing a brain with me.

-Mary Burkart, Murrieta, 2010

About the Authors

Daniel Novak has worked as an instructional designer and multimedia developer in the public sector, private sector, and academia. He will begin doctoral study in Education at the University of Washington in 2010. You can contact him at: **Daniel@InstructionalDeveloper.com.**

Mary Burkart has worked as an instructional designer, school teacher, and trainer for more than 20 years. You can contact her at: **Mary@InstructionalDeveloper.com**

TABLE OF CONTENTS

CHAPTER 9 QUIZZES AND QUESTION SLIDES 167

CHAPTER 10 PRE-PUBLISHING 177

CHAPTER 11 PUBLISHING YOUR PROJECT 197

NEW IN CAPTIVATE 5

SECTION 508 ACCESSIBILITY

PROFESSIONAL TIPS AND TRICKS

Chapter 1
The Rapid Development Process

In this chapter

This chapter will provide you with essential information for rapid development and design using Adobe Captivate 5 including:

- eLearning Design using Captivate 5
- eLearning development software
- Rapid prototyping model
- Stages of rapid design
- 508 compliance principles

Introduction

Learning professionals (like you) are under constant pressure to produce eLearning materials in shorter and shorter timeframes. You have client review deadlines, user acceptance tests, and SME meetings to conduct. On top of all that, you need to build in time to look at new eLearning development tools and evaluate new ways to improve your development processes. With all of this pressure, when will you ever find the time to learn Adobe's latest edition of Captivate? Answer: Right now.

Welcome to **Rapid Development with Adobe Captivate 5 for Windows**! While this book is not exhaustive, it will help you establish confidence in your Captivate skills. We aim to provide you with **Just Enough** information to start your project, animate it, and publish it with professional-caliber results. With this book, you'll become very comfortable with Captivate 5.

As multimedia instructional designers in a major corporation, the authors know how hard it can be to learn new software. We also know that programs like Captivate 5 can help you reduce your eLearning development and production time. Our book is full of settings, examples, ideas, and processes that can help you save time and minimize your development efforts.

In this book, you'll learn how to

- Use rapid development techniques
- Set up Captivate 5
- Record your screenshots
- Add multimedia content
- Create reusable components
- Comply with Section 508 Accessibility guidelines
- Make assessments
- Publish and deploy your project

Let's kick off this book with a brief look at some of the recent trends in instructional design and training development.

How to Use This Book

The authors wrote this book because of the lack of practically useful books on Captivate 5 development on the market. We wanted to write a book that you could pick up and use immediately, a book that you can rely on as you deal with Captivate's learning curve. To that end, we tried to keep this book practical and grounded in our experience as instructional designers at a Fortune 500 corporation.

To get the most out of this book, read through it once to get a sense of the possibilities and complexities of Adobe Captivate. Add a few Post-It notes to help you remember settings and hot keys.

After you've read through it once, keep the book close at hand while you work and practice in Captivate. Refer to the book's table of contents and the index to help you find the answers that you need.

Also, keep an eye open for the following icons that we've placed throughout the text:

 NEW: This indicates features that are new to Captivate 5.

 PRO-TIPS: These are professional tips and tricks drawn from the authors' experience.

 Accessibility TIPS: This is information about how to make your Captivate projects accessible to persons with disabilities. These tips comply with Section 508 Standards.

eLearning Design in Adobe Captivate 5

You've determined that there is an instructional need in your organization. Now you'll have to decide how to address it.

As you start to lay out your eLearning materials in Captivate 5, you should consider whether you should build **Courses**, **Training**, or **Performance Support** to bridge your learning gap. Each of these instructional strategies requires a different kind of product. In the table below, we compare the defining qualities of each strategy and Captivate's role in your project.

Instructional Strategies	Defining Qualities	Captivate's Role
Courses	Courses typically build knowledge and skills over several stand-alone lessons. They are best used when learner skills need to be built from a very low level to a very high level.	Captivate will allow you to design, develop, and publish your eLearning courses. It also includes tools that can aggregate your individual projects into courses and track your learners progress through a Learning Management System (LMS)
Training	Training takes place before learners have to perform their tasks. This is most often used to teach conceptual or abstract knowledge that must be transferred to a specific task later.	You can use Captivate's branching features to create take learners through complex scenarios. You can also combine your multimedia resources into Captivate to engage the learner's attention. This will help learners accomplish far-transfer tasks.
Performance Support	Performance support materials are there to help users as they perform their tasks. Very short and to the point, these lessons focus on helping users accomplish tasks that they already understand (but may have forgotten).	You can use Captivate to develop short screen capture movies that can help users perform complicated tasks on computers. You can also use interactive objects to help learners move through complicated decision pathways.

eLearning Development Software

Adobe Captivate 5 is widely used, well documented, and very powerful. However, there are other kinds of eLearning development tools and solutions on the market.

We recommend that you consider some of the following questions before you select Captivate or any other tool for your project.

1. Is the cost of the tool an important factor in your selection?

eLearning software packages vary widely in cost, from hundreds to thousands of dollars. You may want to check the price tag before making a decision.

> *Why Captivate? Captivate is not cheap, but it is definitely a worthwhile investment. Its feature set is quite broad, and it has the potential to reduce your development time and save you money!*

2. Will you need to customize or brand the user's interface?

Many clients require that their learning materials and performance support tools have a uniform look and feel. They may ask you to repurpose their existing PowerPoint layouts for your project, use the company's logo and colors, or restrict the replay controls on the finished product.

Each piece of eLearning development software allows for different levels of customization. You may want to consider how strictly your client would like to control or brand the user's experience before selecting a piece of software.

> *Why Captivate? As we will show you in this book, Captivate can provide you with substantial opportunities to customize and brand your courses, training modules, or promotional movies.*
>
> *Also, Captivate 5 makes it easier than ever to develop reusable branded templates for your project.*

3. Will you need to capture media?

Many eLearning authoring products take precise screen captures of users' actions. Some even copy the output text and icons from the software that you are capturing. If you will need to capture examples of exemplary users at work, you will want to favor this feature.

The idea of 'capturing' extends beyond screenshots. Many performance support software packages will capture images, audio, video, and PowerPoint slides in addition to screenshots. As you review your options, think about what kinds of media you will need to include in your final product.

> *Why Captivate? Captivate can help you capture, organize, and reuse your screen shots. Capturing software procedures can help you preserve, centralize, and disseminate your organization's tribal knowledge.*
>
> *Captivate 5 also accepts a larger array of media than ever! As we show you in this book, Captivate is a hub for all kinds of multimedia of media. Images, audio, video, and interactive segments can be chained together seamlessly.*

4. Do you want to include interactive features in your product?

Interactivity is a major feature of many eLearning development tools. Some of the software tools will allow your users to click, scroll, drag, or mouse-over specific spots to proceed through a simulation or reveal more information.

If interactivity is not important to you, you may select a less complex tool, such as static web pages (created in Dreamweaver or a content management system like WordPress) or PowerPoint presentations that display your content.

> *Why Captivate? Captivate has an array of interactive objects that can enhance the end user's learning experience. Click boxes, rollover boxes, and branching projects can get the learner involved with your content.*

5. Is the file format of the final product important to your client?

Performance support software can export your product to a number of formats, including CDs, Microsoft Word, and (most commonly) Flash.

Your client may need you to export your product to a specific format in order to work with their learning management system or intranet. You may want to ask them for details about how they will deploy your support tools so that you can choose a software package with the necessary features.

If your client doesn't have an answer, you might have to provide a deployment plan for them. Once you come up with a plan, ask around in your IT department to feel out potential pitfalls.

> **Why Captivate?** *Captivate 5 can output your project into a number of formats, including Flash (SWF), Adobe PDF, and Microsoft Word.*

6. Will you need to change or update your product more than a few times per year?

You may want to consider how often you will have to make changes to the final product when evaluating eLearning software. Some authoring tools make it easier to update your products than others.

> **Why Captivate?** *You can create easily maintained eLearning objects in Captivate through the use of Master Slides and templates. We'll show you this process in a later chapter.*

7. Are the availability of technical support and access to a developer community important to you?

Some authoring tools have larger developer communities and better technical support than others. You may want to visit the software maker's website and visit their help forums before making a decision. If you still can't determine if they provide enough support, don't be afraid to call them and see for yourself.

Why Captivate? Adobe's tech support, help, and user forums are excellent sources of information on the product, but Captivate's large developer community produces a lot of excellent Captivate training, tricks, and troubleshooting techniques.

8. Are the software's ease-of-use and learning curve decisive factors?

If your project has a short production cycle, you and your team may not have time to learn a complex piece of software. A simpler, more targeted piece of software may fit your needs. Experiment with available tools to find the perfect mixture of features and ease of use.

Why Captivate? There's no denying that Captivate has a learning curve, but you have this book! We're going to help you get through the initial learning curve of Captivate by teaching you common tasks that you'll need to perform while designing and constructing your projects. You'll also find:

1 • Capture Slides with Subject Matter Experts

2 • Edit Captured Slides for Continuity

3 • Add Script to Slide Notes

4 • Publish as Word Doc for SME Review

5 • Text-to-Speech and Objects

6 • Publish Your Prototype for Client Review

7 • Polishing and Deployment

8 • Evaluation and Further Development

A Rapid Prototyping Model of eLearning Development in Captivate 5

The world of eLearning changes constantly, with new eLearning technologies emerging all the time. These programs can provide us with new workflow and development opportunities. As learning professionals, we must capitalize on those opportunities to improve our design and development processes.

Captivate 5 is not just a piece of software. It is a tool that provides the framework for a **Rapid Prototype** process. This process can allow learning professionals to provide instructional products faster, cheaper, and at a higher quality.

This section of the chapter will take you through the processes and roles that you will need to understand in order to take full advantage of Captivate 5's robust features. If you follow this model and the information in this book, you will spend less of your time in Captivate development and more time designing, testing, and improving your products.

Stages of Development

Once you have completed a preliminary task and audience analysis, you should start moving towards your first prototype as quickly as possible. The graphic on the previous page summarizes the process as we see it. Let's take a closer look at each stage.

1. **Capture Slides with the Subject Matter Expert (SME).** Use this opportunity to get the information out of the SME's head and into your Captivate project. Often, you will be capturing the SME's expertise using software, sit the SME down at your desk and have them perform their tasks while Captivate records the screen. You can move more quickly through your captures if your SME has already set up an example data set or project.

   Make sure to use the **Capture Pause Hotkey (Pause)** if your SME wanders off track, or if you need to reset your example data. This will prevent Captivate from capturing undesired slides that you will have to weed out later.

   Also, you may want to consider using a **Remote Desktop** tool to help you capture your images. If you configure the technology properly, you can use Remote Desktop software to view your SMEs desktop computer. This will allow you to capture their computer's screen without installing Captivate on their system.

 ## PRO-TIP: Knowledge Capture

You should try to capture as much of your SME's knowledge as you can. For example, try audio recording your initial discussions for later transcription. You can then use these transcriptions to help prepare your script

2. **Edit Captured Slides for Continuity.**
   Immediately begin weeding out your incorrect or duplicate slides while your SME is on hand. They can help you spot errors in continuity and fill in missing steps. As you review your captures, put placeholders for your non-screenshot content slides into your project to help break the captures into chunks.

 ## PRO-TIP: Avoiding Missing Captures

Captivate can sometimes miss capturing a slide, especially in Internet Explorer. If this happens, you can go back and recapture that missing slide and add it back into the slide order. To avoid missed captures, click through the process slowly, listen for the 'capture' sound, let each screen fully load before clicking, and use the manual capture hotkeys to manually take a screenshot.

3. **Add Script to Slide Notes.** Go through your captured process carefully one more time with your SME. Have them narrate the screen shots as you type their comments into the slide notes. This is a good way to use your time together.

4. **Publish as Word Doc for SME Review.** After your SME has gone back to their usual work, go back through your script one more time in Captivate. Then, use the **Publish as Word Doc** function to export the video as a text/still image document. You can then email this to your SME for review. Ask them to use **Track Changes** in Word to ensure that you can easily see their changes in the script.

5. **Text-to-Speech and Objects.** Once your SMEs have reviewed your script, you can turn on the text-to-speech voices, then, add your highlight boxes and other objects to your slides. Then, time up your visual objects to coincide with events in the narration. This will help your clients and stakeholders get a good sense for your movie with minimal extra effort.

6. **Publish Your Prototype for Client Review.** Now that your text-to-speech and object timings are in place, you should publish a rough prototype for your clients. Don't be distressed if they aren't 100% happy with the movie! At this point, you should be aiming for about 50% completion. Incorporate the reviewers' suggestions (if they are relevant), and continue adding or pruning content.

7. **Polishing and Deployment.** Now that your content is settled and you're confident in your script, get a real person to record your narration. You can use the tips in this book to do it yourself, if you like. We've only encountered a few cases where clients have preferred the synthetic voices to human voices, so any natural voiceover will improve your product at this point. Also, you'll want to configure your user interface, review the finished project a few times, and then publish the product for final inspection by the client.

8. **Evaluation and Further Development.** Though your clients pay the bills, your job isn't done until you've run at least one round of user acceptance or end-user testing. You can learn a lot of unexpected things from watching learners use your product, so take some time to do some observation. Then, go back and incorporate any useful feedback and republish again.

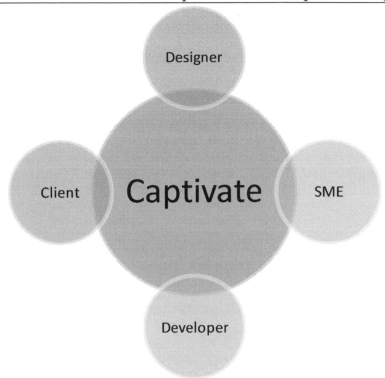

Captivate as Development Facilitator

One of the most unique things about Captivate 5 as a software package is the way that it facilitates a whole range of contributor roles, including Designer, SME, Developer, and Client. You may find yourself acting in more than one of these roles. You might even play all four roles at once in some projects! Let's look at how each role contributes to the final product:

- **Designer.** An instructional designer's core concerns are order and sequence. Captivate helps developers capture, chunk, and sequence their projects very quickly. Also, it provides the designer with many opportunities for formative feedback from the SME and Client.
- **SME.** Subject Matter Experts are invaluable sources of information about your topic. If you are building technical training outside of your field of knowledge, your SME might be your only window into the end user's world. It is important that you select or request SMEs that you trust will provide accurate information. Your goal is to bottle their knowledge and experience, then present it to users in a digestible form.
- **Developer.** Once the Designer and SME are happy with their content, the Developer can begin to enhance the visual and multimedia components of

the project. Developers can use Captivate to house their video, advanced actions, widgets, and Flash animations. Captivate 5 is more closely integrated with Adobe Photoshop, Adobe Flash, and Techsmith Camtasia than ever before! Remember: the most successful projects involve developers early and receive input from them frequently.

- **Client.** You should periodically provide your client with opportunities to evaluate your project. We recommend getting feedback at two points: when you conduct your SME review of your script, and again after you publish your movie with text-to-speech. These two stages are at crucial junctures in the project. Getting feedback from your clients at these points will reduce the potential for cascading changes to your project.

PRO-TIP: Review Your Project with the Customer

Make sure that you come up with a way for your client to make comments about your work. You can provide your client with the Adobe AIR Captivate Reviewer or a Word doc version of your project. At the very least, provide them with some sort of Change Request Form that records the desired change, its slide number, and any changes to the voiceover. (You can make this form easily in Excel.)

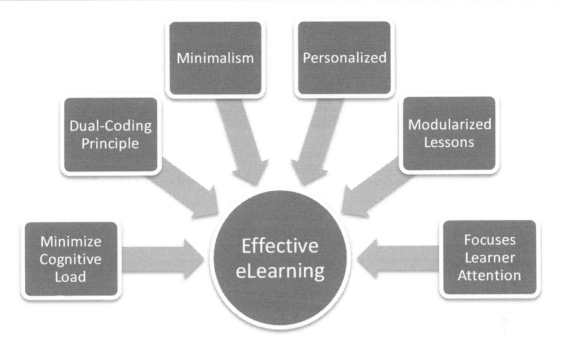

Design Principles for Effective eLearning

As we noted earlier, Captivate is only a tool that supports a development process. In addition to learning about this tool and process, you should educate yourself about some of the current trends in instructional design. The more you know about these recent trends, the better your final product!

Let's explore five key **Design Principles for Effective eLearning:**

- **Minimize Cognitive Load.** A person's short-term memory is finite, and placing too many things on screen at once can divide peoples' attention very easily. Avoid complex animations, distracting images, or anything unrelated to the task at hand. Avoid putting too much text onscreen. Instead, put a visual image onscreen and use audio narration to tell the story. Text is a poor substitute for a picture, graph, or table.

  You should also employ a technique called **Progressive Disclosure** to help manage your learners' cognitive load. Instead of showing long, bulleted paragraphs on your slides, read the bulk of the text in your narration. Display only short, key-word bullets on the slide itself. Then reveal the bullets one at a time, as the voiceover says the words. Make sure that the words in the bullets are identical to the words in the voiceover.

- **Dual-Coding Principle.** Some people think that audio narration is distracting to learners. This is untrue, though it does sap learner attention when used incorrectly. However, cognitive scientists have shown that learners perform much better when they hear audio narration that reinforces visual stimuli (and vice-versa).

  In practice, this means that you must keep your audio in synch with your video, and your narration must match any text on the screen very closely. Use animation sparingly to minimize cognitive load, but do use it at key moments to help reinforce the dual coding of audio- and visual-memory.

- **Minimalism.** With all of the fancy features and multimedia gadgets in Captivate 5, there exists a temptation to use them all in your projects. You should try to restrain this impulse, because an excess of multimedia objects and text can create unnecessary cognitive load for the user. Instead, prefer modest, clear, instructionally effective graphics to flashy movies. Your end project may not look as flashy, but your learners will retain more of the information if you reduce distracting features from your product.

  In the spirit of minimalism, look for ways to reduce the amount of content that you include in your movies, or break the content across several movies. Ask your SMEs (and yourself!) if the information is 'need-to-know' or 'nice-to-know.' This will help you avoid confusing the users with a barrage of information that is not relevant to their current task.

- **Personalized.** Personalized eLearning has three qualities:
  1. Some degree of **user control**. Allowing users to move back and forth through your slides, creating branching lessons, and providing a table of contents can go far in helping your learners stay engaged with your materials
  2. Use of the **Personalization Principle**. Instead of writing in passive voice, write directly to your learners. Use simple, conversational-style language to help them follow along. Address them directly as 'you,' and talk about the tasks that 'we' must do. Pretend that you are in the room with them as you guide them through an activity, and then write the script with that same level of informal ease.
  3. The use of **Agents**. Agents are fictional (or real) 'people' that guide your learner through a lesson. You can create an agent by placing a still image or a short movie of a person into your project. Putting a friendly face in the training makes the eLearning experience more engaging for learners. It also makes them more likely to complete their lessons.

- **Modularized Lessons.** Break your lessons into small parts. This will give users more control over the content that they can select. You should help the user get to the information that they want as quickly and easily as possible. This can also reduce development and maintenance times if you use templates.

- **Focuses Learner Attention.** You should use highlight boxes, zoom boxes, and other visual means of focusing your learners' attention on the important things onscreen. You can also use audio cues to help the user keep track of the action onscreen. For example, you can use a highlight box to emphasize important features as you also direct the learner where to look (i.e. "You'll see that the option is in the upper-right hand corner."). Without visual and auditory cues from you, the learner might miss the important parts of the movie.

Section 508 Compliance

Imagine turning off your monitor, unplugging you mouse, and deactivating your soundcard. Could you still access the Web without seeing, hearing, or touching the computer? For a great number of people across the globe who live with disabilities, navigating the Internet is a very real challenge.

In 1998, Congress made changes to the Rehabilitation Act requiring federal agencies to ensure that electronic and information technology on the Web was accessible to people with disabilities. In essence, Section 508 requires agencies to give disabled users access to information that is equivalent to the access available to persons that do not have disabilities.

Many people who use the web have one or more disabilities, as defined in the 508 standards. These can include:

- Blindness, color blindness, or weak vision

- Deafness or hardness of hearing

- Physical disabilities that affect motor control

- Inability to use a mouse

- Photosensitivity epilepsy that can trigger a seizure from computer screen movement

This law applies to all Federal agencies that develop or use Intranet/Internet-based resources. However, a recent movement in the developer community is pushing to include accessibility for electronic and information technology in the private sector. Regardless of the context, when technology is not made accessible, people with disabilities have difficulty obtaining and using information on the Internet. The purpose of Section 508 is to eliminate usability barriers in information technology.

This section will give you an overview of this information. It is drawn from information from the Web Accessibility Initiative, which can be found on the Web at http://www.w3.org.

Four Principles of Design for Accessibility

The accessibility guidelines below are structured around four principles that will ideally make the Web accessible to everyone. A complete explanation of the 508 Guidelines can be accessed at http://www.w3.org.

- **Perceivable** – You must present information and user interface components in ways that disabled users can perceive. In other words, interface information and components on a Web page cannot be undetectable to all of their senses. A few specific guidelines:

  1. Text Alternatives: Provide text alternatives for any non-text content so that it can be changed into other forms people need, such as large print, Braille, speech, symbols, or simpler language
  2. Time-based Media: Provide alternatives for time-based media.
  3. Adaptable: Create content that can be presented in different ways (for example a simpler layout) without losing information or structure.
  4. Distinguishable: Make it easier for users to see and hear content including separating foreground from background.

- **Operable** – The user must be able to operate all interface components and navigation. This means that users must be able to operate the interface if they have vision, motor-coordination, or hearing disabilities.

  1. Keyboard Accessible: Make all functionality available from a keyboard.
  2. Enough Time: Provide users enough time to read and use content.
  3. Seizures: Do not design content in a way that is known to cause seizures.
  4. Navigable: Provide ways to help users navigate, find content, and determine where they are.

- **Understandable** - Information and the operation of user interface must be understandable by the end-user. This means that users must be able to understand the information as well as the operation of the user interface.

  1. Readable: Make text content readable and understandable.
  2. Predictable: Make Web pages appear and operate in predictable ways.
  3. Input Assistance: Help users avoid and correct mistakes.

- **Robust** - Content must be in a robust enough format that it can be interpreted reliably by a wide range of user agents, including browsers and assistive technologies such as screen readers. This means that users should be able to access the content as assistive technologies change,

  1. Compatible: Maximize compatibility with current and future user agents, including assistive technologies.

Several documents are available online to help you develop with 508-compliance in mind:

- Authoring Tool Accessibility Guidelines (ATAG) 2.0. This can be found at the website: http://www.w3.org.

- Using Adobe Captivate 5. This PDF can be found at the web address: http://help.adobe.com/en_US/captivate/cp/using/captivate_5_help.pdf

Captivate 5 and Section 508 Standards

Adobe has taken the appropriate steps to make sure all Captivate 5 projects can conform to Section 508 standards. We have included information about how Captivate 5 conforms to these standards. You will find a special icon in this book to help you identify areas where you use Captivate 5 to help you make 508-compliant videos.

The following Adobe Captivate elements are accessible when the **Enable Accessibility** box (in the **Preferences | Publish Settings** menu) above is checked:

- Project name and Project description are derived from Project Properties

- Slide accessibility text and Slide label are derived from Slide Properties

- The function of Buttons and Playback controls are read by screen readers

- If an Adobe Captivate SWF file is password protected, the prompt for a password is read by screen readers

- Titles, question, answers, button text, and scoring report on Quiz Question Slides are read by screen readers

  We will cover these options in greater depth during the course of the book.

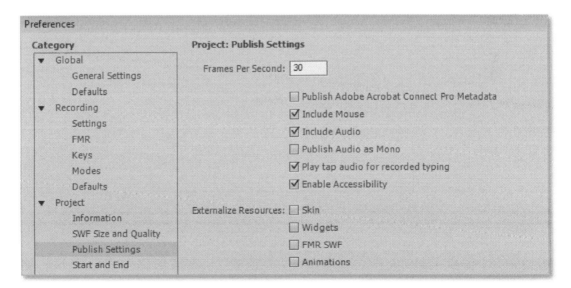

Read These Books

While this book will help you learn a new eLearning development tool, it does not contain everything you'll need to know to create quality eLearning materials. You should consult the sources below to develop a greater understanding of current developments in instructional design, cognitive science, visual communication, and education.

Clark, R. C. (2007). *Developing Technical Training: A Structured Approach for Developing Classroom and Computer-based Instructional Materials.* San Francisco: Pfeiffer.

Clark, R. C., & Chopeta, L. (2004). *Graphics for Learning.* San Francisco, CA: Pfeiffer.

Clark, R. C., & Mayer, R. E. (2007). *e-Learning and the Science of Instruction: Proven Guidelines for Consumers and Designers of Multimedia Learning.* San Francisco: Pfeiffer.

Duarte, N. (2008). *Slide:ology - The Art and Science of Creating Great Presentations.* Sebastapol, CA: O'Reilly Media.

Edmundson, A. (2007). *Globalized E-Learning Cultural Challenges.* Hershey, PA: Information Science Publishing.

Horton, W. K. (2006). *eLearning by Design.* San Francisco: Peiffer.

Keller, J. M. (1999). Motivation in Cyber Learning Environments. *International Journal of Educational Technology* , 7-30.

Kirkpatrick, D. L. (2006). *Evaluating Training Programs: The Four Levels (3rd Edition).* San Francisco: Berrett-Koehler.

Lakoff, G., & Johnson, M. (1999). *Philosophy in the Flesh: The Embodied Mind and Its Challenge to Western Thought.* New York: Basic Books.

Mager, R. F. (1997). *Analyzing Performance Problems, Third Edition.* Atlanta, GA: CEP Press.

Mager, R. F. (1997). *Preparing Instructional Objectives, Third Edition.* Atlanta, GA: CEP Press.

McLuhan, M. (2004). *Understanding Media: The Extensions of Man.* Boston, MA: The MIT Press.

McLuhan, M., & Fiore, Q. (1967). *The Medium is the Massage: An Inventory of Effects.* New York: Bantam Books.

Reynolds, G. (2008). *Presentation Zen.* Berkeley, CA: New Riders.

Rossett, A. (1998). *First Things Fast: A Handbook for Performance Analysis.* San Francisco: Pfeiffer.

Rossett, A., & Schafer, L. (2007). *Job Aids and Performance Support: Moving From Knowledge in the Classroom to Knowledge Everywhere.* San Francisco: Pfeiffer.

Thiagarajan, S. (1999, October 1). *Rapid Instructional Design.* Retrieved July 10, 2010, from Thiagi.com: http://www.thiagi.com/article-rid.html

Tufte, E. R. (2006). *The Cognitive Style of PowerPoint: Pitching Out Corrupts Within.* New York: Graphics Press.

Tufte, E. R. (2001). *The Visual Display of Quantitative Information.* New York: Graphics Press.

Chapter 2
Installation, Workspaces, and Settings

In this chapter

This chapter will provide you with all the information you will need to get started with Adobe Captivate 5 including:

- Downloading and installing Captivate 5
- Starting a new custom project
- Setting up and understanding the workspace
- Setting up preferences

Downloading Adobe Captivate 5

You can download Adobe® Captivate® 5 from
http://www.adobe.com/products/captivate.

Make sure you download the appropriate version of Captivate 5 (PC or Mac, as well as the right language).

Also, make sure you download and install the **NeoSpeech™** and **Loquendo™** Text-to-Speech voices. These voice databases come as two separate files, so make sure to download and install both! They will come in handy later

If you have a serial number, you can enter it during the installation process.

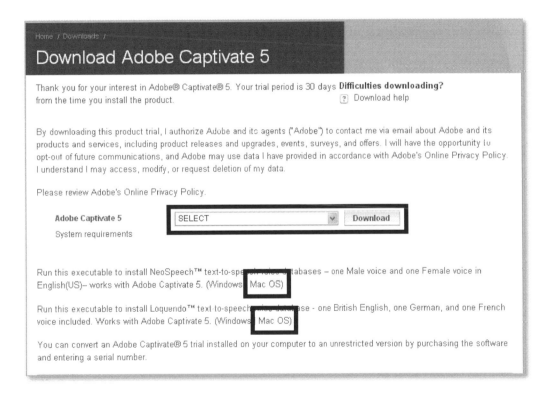

Installing Adobe Captivate 5

After downloading the installation file, you can double-click the .exe to begin the installation process. The image below will take you on a quick, visual tour of the Captivate 5 installation process.

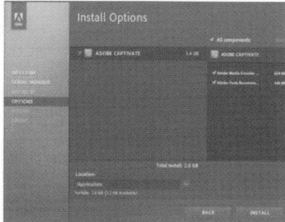

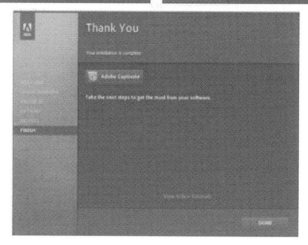

Installation Tips

Installing Captivate 5 is a fairly straightforward process, and you will most likely install the software without any problems. However, users sometimes encounter errors in the installation. If the Captivate 5 installer reports an error, try some of the following troubleshooting tips:

- If Captivate won't install because of your computer's resolution, raise your resolution to 1024x768 (or higher).
- If the Captivate installer asks you to close a program to continue the installation, save your work in that program and close it.
- Try installing Captivate 5 into a subdirectory in your Program Files folder (i.e. /Program Files/CP5/)
- If you still can't get it to work, consult Adobe's support materials that come included on the Captivate 5 CD, or Adobe's online help system.
- Ask your IT professional for help, especially if you work in a secured network.
- Adobe's developer forums and website are excellent resources for advanced troubleshooting and help:
  http://forums.adobe.com/community/adobe_captivate

These tips can help you dodge some of the more common installation problems. You can always contact Adobe's customer support system through Adobe.com if you find yourself really stuck.

Running Captivate 5

If Captivate 5 installed correctly, the launch screen above will appear. After a few seconds, the Captivate window will load, and you'll see a screen like the one below:

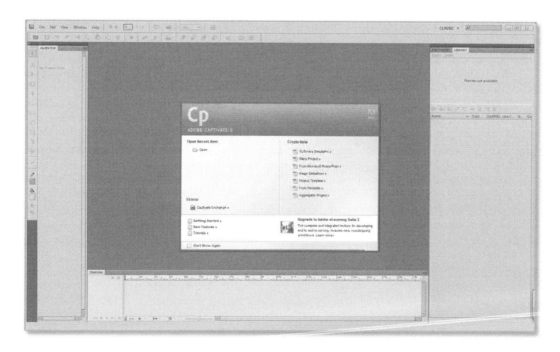

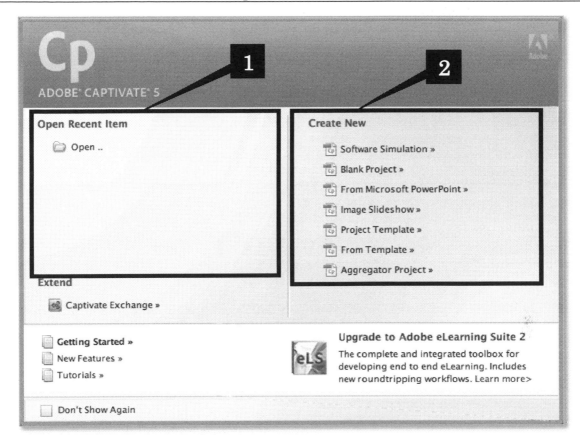

Main Project Window

The Main Project window is at the center of the first screen you'll see when you open Captivate, and many of your future projects will begin here.

1. The **Open Recent Item** column on the left keeps track of your recently used projects and templates.
2. The **Create New** column on the right provides you with quick access to a number of project types and configurations. Over the next few chapters, we'll show you how to select, customize, and develop these basic project types into high-quality learning objects.

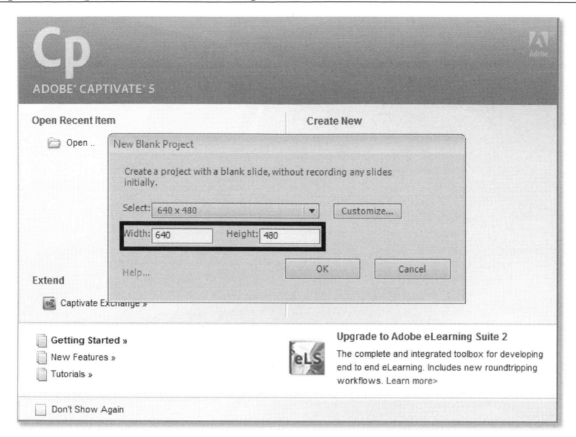

Setting up a custom project

To get things rolling, we selected the **New Blank Project** window from the **Create New** menu.

You can use blank projects for a number of different purposes. You can use them as a storyboarding tool, a canvas to arrange your elements, or as a clean slate for another project template.

There are really two options available for customization here. The **Select** drop-down menu allows you to choose from a series of predefined sizes. You can also use the **Width and Height boxes** to set a custom size for the project. In this case, we're choosing a large, roughly 4:3 slide area.

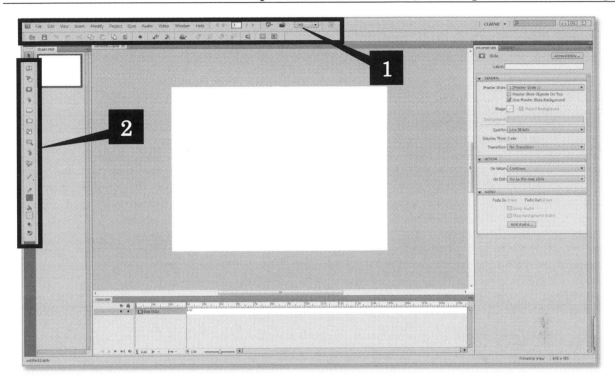

Setting Up Your Workspace

5 NEW: Workspaces

Adobe has completely rebuilt Captivate's interface for version 5.

1. If you're familiar with Captivate from past versions, you'll find many familiar features in the **menu bar at the top of the screen**.
2. If you're new to Captivate, you'll find that the new interface is very similar to Adobe's other products, such as Photoshop and Illustrator. Many of the visual metaphors are the same, especially the **toolbar on the far left**.

Regardless of your level of Captivate experience, this new interface is very powerful, and comes with new opportunities and new pitfalls. As with all workspaces, the **'Classic Workspace'** requires a little customization to reach its full potential. We encourage you to find ways to arrange your workspace to fit your workflow. To get you started, we'll show you how we like to set up our workspaces.

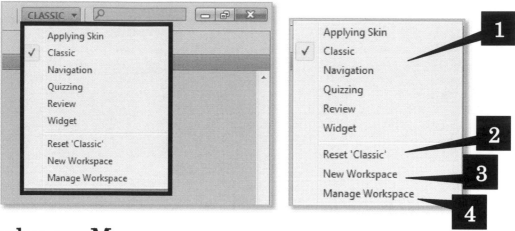

The Workspace Menu

You'll find the Workspace Menu in the upper-right corner of the Captivate window. This menu allows you to do four things:

1. **Access existing workspace layouts.** Adobe has provided several layouts to you based on tasks you might perform, such as applying a skin or working on quizzes. Try them out by selecting them from the drop down. You can return to the default view by selecting 'Classic.'
2. **Reset your workspace.** If you rearrange some things but want to return to your workspace's default view, you can click the **'Reset'** option to go back to your last saved state.
3. **Saving a new workspace.** You can use the **'New Workspace'** menu to save the workspace so that you can switch to it at a later time.
4. **Managing your** workspaces. You can use this option to delete or select your workspaces through a menu.

After you get a sense for some of the layouts, try resizing the panels and rearranging the screen. You'll find that your preferences might change with time and tasks, so look for opportunities to reduce the distance that your mouse-hand needs to travel. If you're right handed, try arranging your menus on the right side. If you don't like that, experiment some more until you find a suitable workspace configuration.

You're likely to spend a lot of time in Captivate 5, so get comfortable.

The Windows Panel

After working with Adobe Photoshop for a number of years, the authors find that they like to cluster all of the Window options into a single **Window Panel**. This panel contains almost all of the information that you might need in Captivate.

This configuration does not come premade, so you'll have to construct it yourself. Below, you can see two images.

1. The **Window menu** below is from the Captivate menu bar. You can select one of the windows from the menu and it will appear on the desktop.
2. You can dock several of these menus to create the attractive, simple panel.

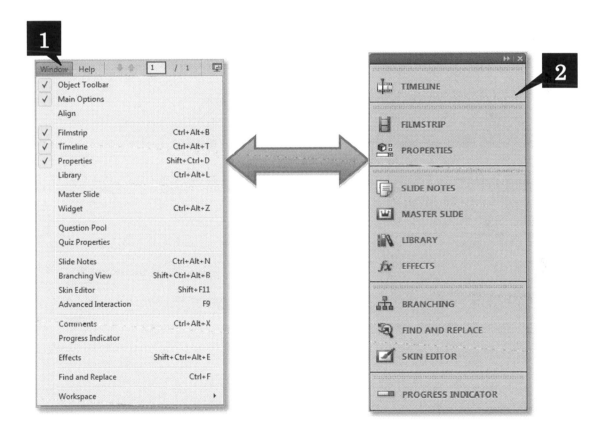

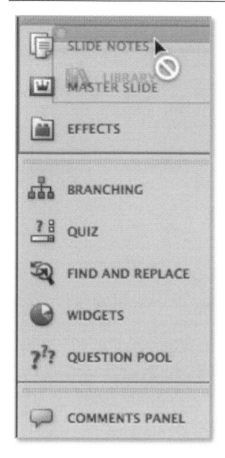

Docking Windows Panels

When you click on one of the windows in the Window menu (i.e. Library), that window will appear in the Captivate interface. If you move that window close to another, they'll stick together. If you look carefully, you'll notice blue lines around the sticky zones. Those will help you see where you panel will land.

In this image, we've already docked several panels together and grouped them by dragging them up and down. Here, we're docking the library to the panel.

Let's take a look at some of the Windows that you'll definitely want to include in your Panel.

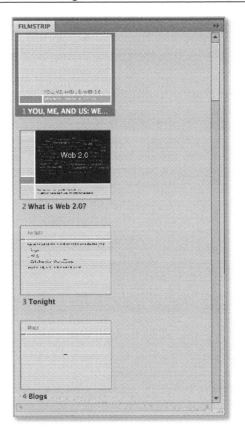

The Filmstrip

The **Filmstrip** shows you thumbnail views of all of the slides in your project. You can use this menu much like the filmstrip in PowerPoint, though it does have some unique properties that we'll explore in context in a later chapter.

You can also drag and stretch the window to view the menu as a **Slide Sorter**.

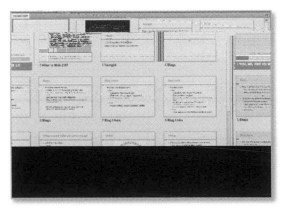

The Timeline

The Timeline is a time-based view of the duration of elements on your slide. Each object is represented as a horizontal 'track,' and time is indicated by the hash marks in the top row. You can zoom in to or out using the slider at the bottom-right of the window.

The moving red line, called the **Playhead**, tells you what point in the slide you're viewing. The stationary red line at the right marks the **End** of the slide.

You can grab the center of an object and drag it to change its start and end time. You can also grab the edges of your objects and drag them to change the object start and end times.

In this screenshot, we have (from bottom to top)

1. Our audio track starting at .5 seconds. The authors like to start their audio tracks .5 seconds after the start of the slide, and end the slide about .5 to 1.5 seconds after the audio finishes. This gives the user a moment to process what they're seeing before the audio starts.
2. Our slide, which lasts for 3.9 seconds
3. A highlight box, which appears at 1.3 seconds
4. The mouse, which moves at 2.6 and clicks at the end. Keep your mouse movements under 2 seconds, as users will get bored watching the mouse crawl across the screen.
   The Red Triangle on the mouse object indicates that the mouse is docked to the slide end. If you increase the slide length, the mouse will move with the end line but will not increase in duration.

The Timeline also displays the layers of slide elements. For example, the mouse in this timeline will appear on top of the highlight box because it is on a higher layer.

This is called the **z-axis order.** You can drag the mouse down to a lower level to have the highlight box appear on top of the mouse.

A Note on Timing

The timing of your objects really makes a difference in the quality of your final project. Good timing can do a lot to improve the quality and effectiveness of your training in some very real ways. The synchronization of audio and visual cues has been empirically shown to guide learner focus and keep their attention.

Notice that our voiceover audio starts a little after the start of the slide. This gives the user a moment to process the screen changes. Also, our highlight box appears in sync with the audio so that it appears just as the narrator mentions the field it highlights. This crisp synchronization reinforces the information in the user's mind, creating a stronger memory.

If you're on a deadline, we recommend spending more time on tuning your project timing than on fancy animations and special effects. The more you practice, the less time it will take you to synchronize your objects. Your learners will thank you!

 ## PRO-TIP: Timing Shortcuts

Here are some handy timing related short cuts. **Display for Rest of Slide** means that once the highlight box appears, it will on the screen for the rest of the slide. If you increase the length of the slide, the highlight box's time will automatically increase as well. You can also use the **Sync with Playhead** option to move the selected object to the playhead.

The Space bar is your best friend in Captivate. You can use the space bar to start and stop your slide's play without clicking the tiny play button on the timeline. You can use this to increase the precision of your timing by pressing the space bar when you hear the first syllable of the related voiceover.

- **Ctrl-E – Display for Rest of Slide**
- **Ctrl-L – Sync with Playhead**
- **Space bar – Start/stop the movie without a mouse**

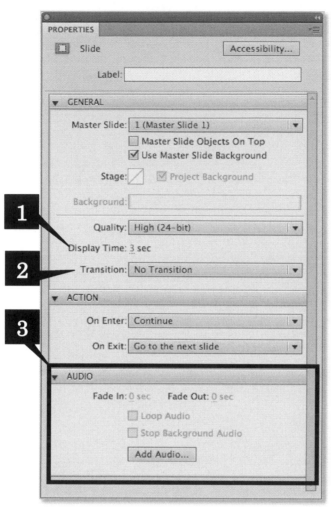

5 NEW: Properties Inspector

In previous versions of Captivate, you would have to double click on an object to see its properties. Captivate 5 now has a universal, context-sensitive menu that automatically displays the properties of any object that you select.

Almost all slides and objects include:

1. **Display Time** option. This is the length of time that a slide or object will stay onscreen.
2. **Transition** options. This allows you to select the transitions or fades that will occur on your slide or object.
3. **Audio** menu. You can add audio tracks to slides or objects through this menu.

We'll take you through object-specific preferences in a later chapter.

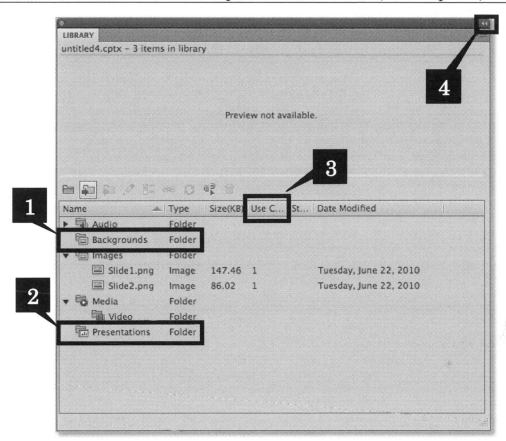

Library Options

The **Library** contains all of the audio, screenshots **(Backgrounds) (1)**, images, movies, and PowerPoint slides **(Presentations) (2)** that you import into your project. Anything you capture or import will automatically be stored here.

You can insert these library items onto any slide. Just navigate to the slide, and then drag the object into position over the slide stage.

You can use the **Use Count (3)** column to identify files that are not in use and clean them from your library, or move them to a new slide. You can also click the title of the column to organize the project by use count. This can make it easier to identify commonly used items.

PRO-TIP: White Arrows

You can use the **white arrows (4)** at the top-right of your panels to keep them 'pinned' open. This is very useful if you need to keep several panels (like Timeline, Filmstrip, and Library) open at the same time.

Library Options

The library has some powerful options. Let's take a closer look at them:

1. **Open Library.** This allows you to open an older project's library and import them into your new project.
2. **Import...** Allows you to import objects to the library.
3. **Export...** Allows you to export library objects to a file.
4. **Edit.** This lets you edit the selected library item.
5. **Properties.** Displays the library item's properties
6. **Usage.** Tells you where this object appears in your project
7. **Update.** If you make changes to an object that you've already imported to your project, you can use this option to automatically import the updated version.
8. **Select Unused Items.** This option selects all of the library objects that you're no longer using. This is a useful, space-saving option. If you delete a bunch of slides from your project, their backgrounds and audio will remain in the library. This button will find the orphaned files. You can then delete them.
9. **Delete.** This permanently deletes the object from your project's library, reducing the project's overall size. Keep in mind that deleting an object from the library does not delete it from your hard drive.

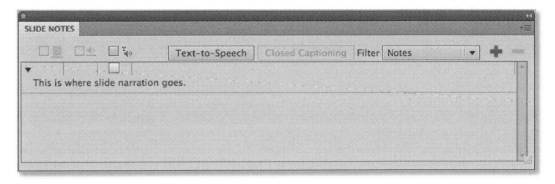

Slide Notes

The **Slide Notes** menu has a number of powerful features that we'll explain in greater depth as we go forward. In their simplest use, slide notes are a great place to manage your script. You can also use them to generate printable Word documents.

We like to use slide notes to storyboard our projects. After we capture our screenshots and prune them, we start typing our narration directly into the slide notes. This allows us to immediately convert our script into **Text-to-Speech (TTS)** audio and get our prototype into review. We'll take you through this process in a later chapter.

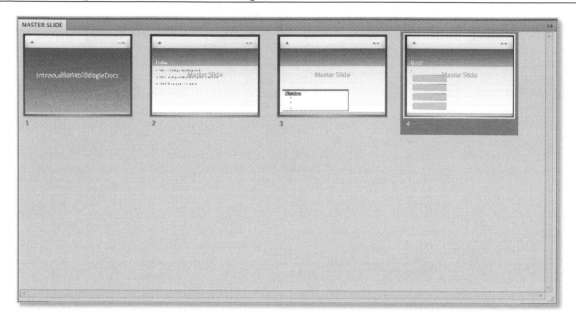

Master Slide

The **Master Slide** window allows you to see and manage your project's master slides. This is a useful window if you have several master slides and you need to quickly refer to their numbers. We'll take you through the ins-and-outs of the Master Slide features in a later chapter.

When you click the Master Slide icon, Captivate will automatically switch you to **Master Slide View**. In this mode, Captivate hides certain objects and properties that are not allowed on Master Slides. To return to your normal project view, click on the Filmstrip icon.

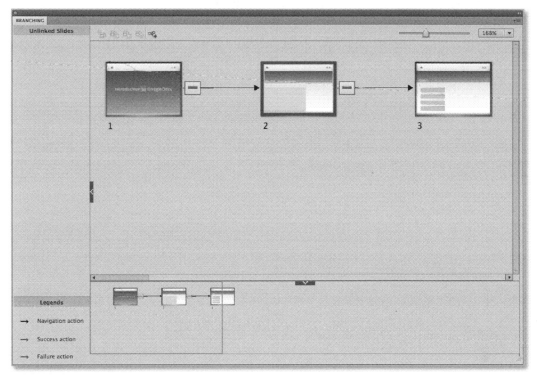

Branching

Branching allows you to give users some agency in their eLearning experience through click boxes and other interactive elements. We'll go into the process of branching later, but you can use it to create custom indexes, develop complex simulations, and map decision points for process analysis.

The **Branching window** shows you a graphic representation of your projects branch points. It also shows your groupings and plots a user's potential paths through a project. Use this menu to make sure that your users wind up where you mean to send them!

This window automatically updates as you add new interactive objects. It is especially handy if you need to quickly make sure that all of your project's pathways are resolved.

We'll discuss branching more in a future chapter.

PRO-TIP: The Maximum Space Layout

Here's a finalized view of the authors' customized 'Maximum Space' layout. The goal of this workspace is to maximize the amount of viewable project space while retaining quick access to options and menus.

If you don't feel like messing around with your workspace just yet, this layout is a good place to start. As you work in Captivate, think about the kinds of tasks that you perform most often, and customize the workspace below to suit those needs. In general, make sure that you are able to see your **Filmstrip**, **Properties Inspector**, **Slide Notes**, and **Library.** A comfortable workspace will make you a happy Captivater!

To get started, make your Captivate screen look like this:

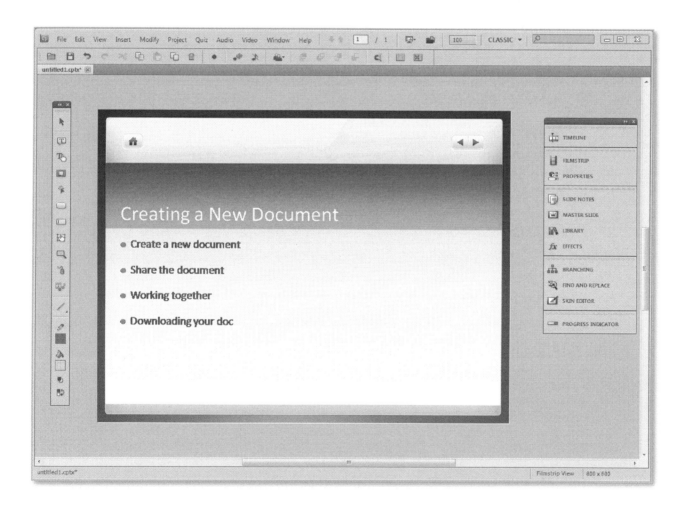

Setting Up Preferences

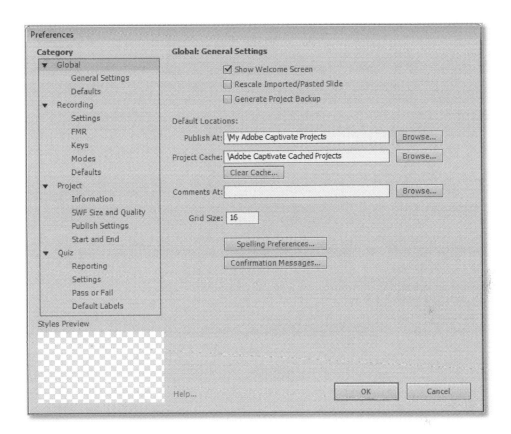

The Preferences Menu

The **Preferences Menu** is home to some of the most important settings in Captivate. Settings these in advance can help you avoid many headaches later in your project. There are dozens of changes to make from this menu, and you'll find yourself tweaking them from project to project.

Let's take a tour of some of the settings that will help you get up and running quickly.

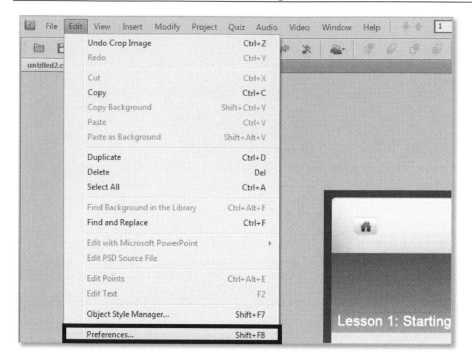

Opening the Preference Window

You can access the preferences window by clicking on the **Edit** menu at the top-left of the screen.

Select **Preferences...** from the drop-down, or use the **Shift+F8** shortcut.

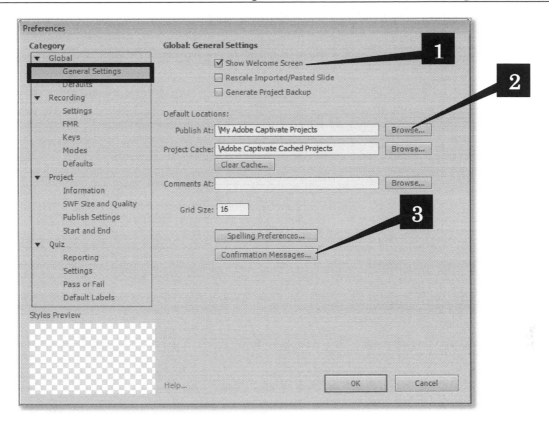

Global General Setting

The General Settings include several important

1. Check the **Show Welcome Screen** setting to show the opening screen each time you open Captivate 5.
2. The **Publish At** setting indicates a default location where your projects are published.
3. You can access the Confirmation Message screen by clicking the **Confirmation Messages** button.

If you do not want this screen to show, check the box on the bottom left corner of the opening window.

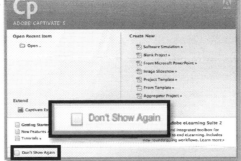

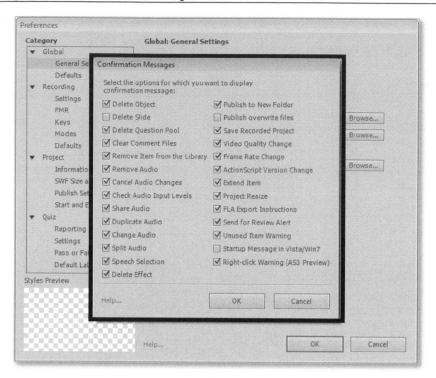

Global Settings Confirmation Messages

Before you make certain changes to your project, Captivate 5 will present you with **Confirmation Messages**. The messages are there to alert you before you do things that can seriously and irreversibly impact your project (i.e. 'Project Resize' or 'Delete Slide'). They are generally quite useful.

Sometimes you may find yourself deleting a number of individual objects, and the frequency of the Confirmation Messages can slow your workflow.

If a Confirmation Message is annoying you, you can always uncheck its box in this menu. You can also check the 'Don't ask me this again' box on the Confirmation Message itself.

If you accidently stop a confirmation message from displaying, you can turn it back on in this menu. This is useful if you want to temporarily stop a message while you delete a series of slides, highlight boxes, or mouse actions from a project.

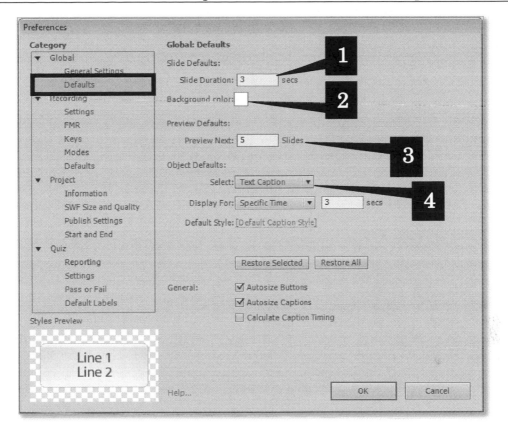

Global Defaults — Object Defaults

There are several useful options in the **Global Defaults** menu.

1. **Slide Duration.** Changing the Slide Duration option can be useful if you want to shorten or lengthen all of the slides in your project. This will also affect the duration of any new slides that you record for your project.
2. **Background Color.** This option allows you to globally change the default background colors for your blank slides.
3. **Preview Next __ Slides**. You can increase or decrease this number to expand or decrease the scope of your previews. Decreasing the number means that your previews will render faster. Increasing the number of slides will give you a better sense of your project's flow.
4. **Object Defaults**. This feature allows you to assign custom defaults for the objects in your project. If you want a highlight box or text caption to appear the same way each time you add them, you can specify that in this set of defaults.

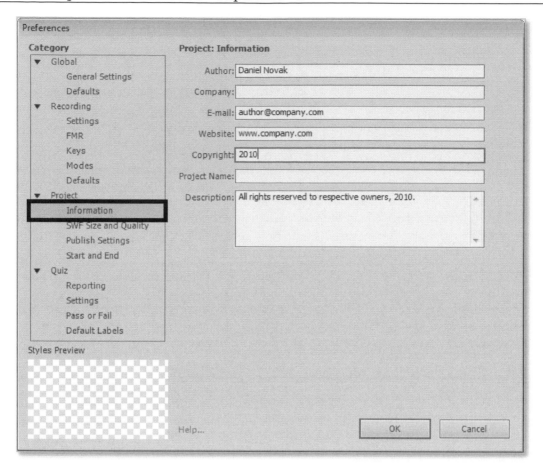

Project Information Preferences

You can enter your project information into this menu. We recommend that you
enter your name, company, and email address if you'd like users to contact you.
Also, enter the year into the copyright field.

Chapter 3
Screen Recording in Captivate 5

In this chapter

This chapter will provide you with all the information you will need to record your projects with Adobe Captivate 5 including:

- Setting Up a Capture
- Defining Project Settings
- Choosing Project Types
- Using Full Motion Recording (FMR) Options

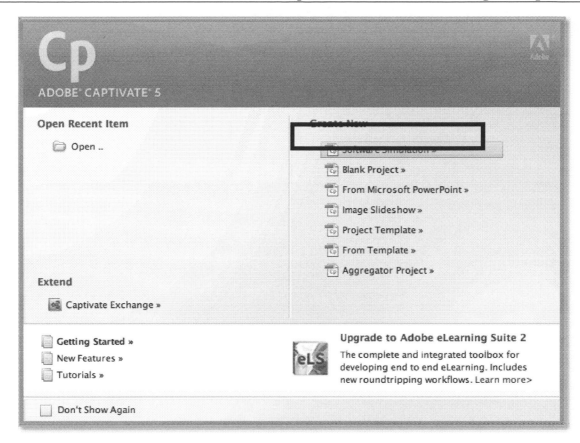

Starting a Software Simulation

Captivate's ability to quickly record screen captures of software is one of the program's most useful features. In this chapter, we're going to take you through the process of setting up a project, recording your slides, and editing the recording.

We'll start by clicking the **Software Simulation** option on the **Create New** menu. This will start the capture engine.

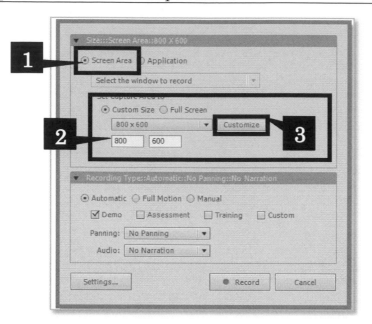

Capturing a Screen Area

When the Capture menu opens, you'll need to choose the size of the screen area that Captivate will capture.

1. Selecting the **Screen Area** radio button will create a red rectangle on your screen, indicating the boundaries of the caption area. You can adjust the size of the rectangle by changing the numbers in the **Set Capture Area to** box.
2. If you enable the **Custom Size** radio button, you can choose a preset size from the drop down menu, or change the capture dimensions manually. You can also select **Full Screen** to capture your entire desktop.
3. If you come up with a custom size that you like and want to use in other projects, you can use the **Customize** button to save it to the drop down list.

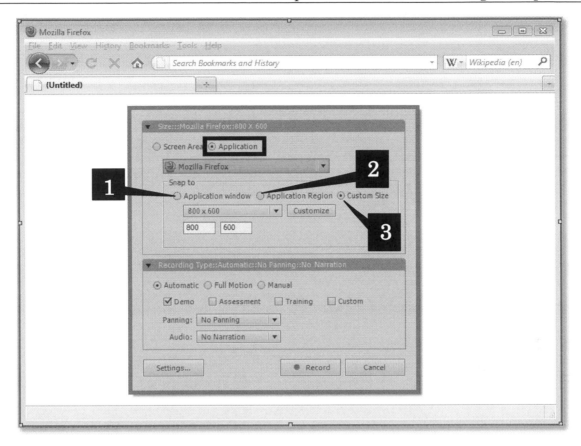

Capturing an Application

You can also click the **Application** radio button to capture a specific program that you have opened. You can select the program from the drop down menu below the radio button.

1. Selecting the **Application window** radio button will cause your red rectangle to snap to the program window and record everything that happens inside of the program.
2. Selecting the **Application Region** radio button will allow you to record the specific region of program that you need.
3. Selecting **Custom Size** will snap your program to fit the size specified in the drop down menu. If you choose 800x600, Captivate will auto-size your program to fit within those boundaries.

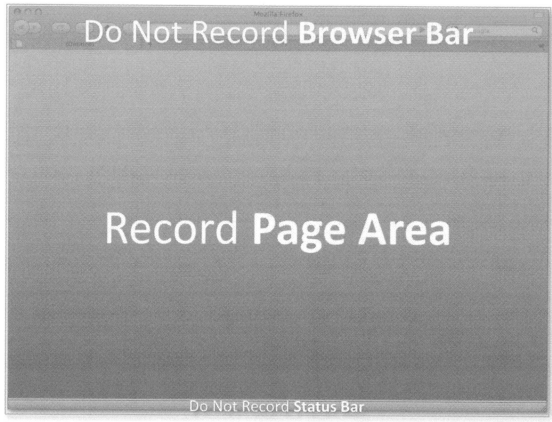

 ## PRO-TIP: Recording a Web Browser

These days, more and more programs are available as Internet-browser-based tools. If you're developing training for a browser-based program, **we recommend that you do not record the browser bar and status bar**. (One exception to this recommendation is if you need to record the typing of a web address in the browser bar.)

Good eLearning shows a program 'realistically' in its proper context. Since your learners will be watching your captures in a browser, there's no need for a second set of browser bars.

Instead, use that screen real estate to capture more of your screen. You can recover 10-20% of the overall screen height by making the browser window larger and moving your red capture rectangle so that it only covers the **Page** area.

You can select just the Page area of a browser capturing setting the Screen Area option to the desired size. Then, resize your browser window until only the page area is within the boundaries of the capture box.

Capture and Object Settings

Before you start a Capture, click the **Settings...** button in the Recording Type menu. This will give us access to some important capture and object settings.

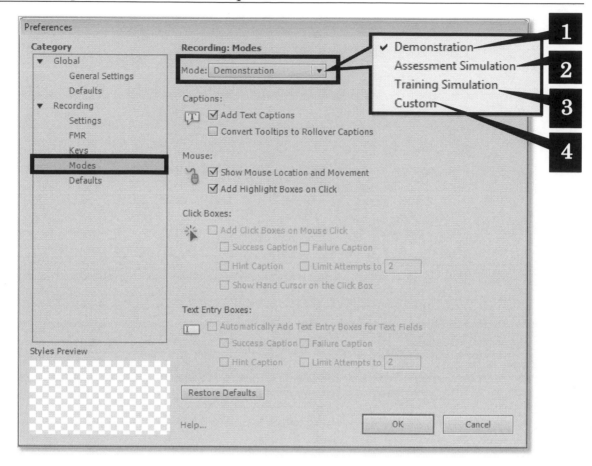

Recording Mode Preferences

This menu allows you to define the kinds of objects that Captivate will automatically add to your project. There are four basic types of capture projects that you can choose from the **Mode** dropdown menu:

1. **Demonstration Mode.** Demonstrations add text captions, highlight boxes, and mouse movement to your screen captures.
2. **Assessment Mode.** Assessments automatically add click boxes and text entry fields with failure text. Captions and mouse movements are left out.
3. **Training Mode.** Training movies are interactive, and include click boxes with hint and failure captions. Captions and mouse movements are left out.
4. **Custom Mode.** Custom mode allows you to choose what Captivate will include by default, and what it will leave out.

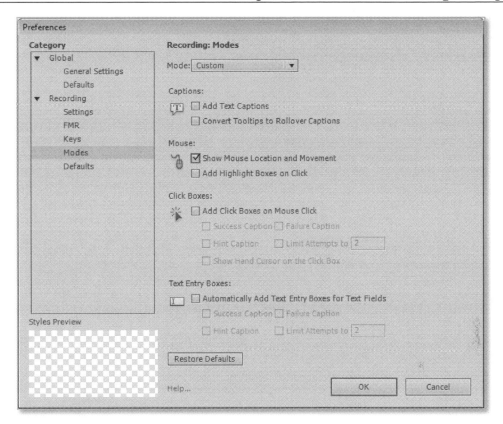

 ## PRO-TIP: Custom Recording Modes

We recommend that you uncheck all default settings except:
Show Mouse Location and Movement.

In most cases, you will want to add text captions, text entry boxes, and click boxes manually. This setup will automatically become your **Custom** mode on the Capture menu.

Keep in mind that Captivate will record your mouse movements no matter what type of project you choose. You can turn the mouse movement option off now, and easily turn it back on later.

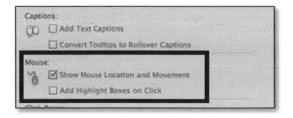

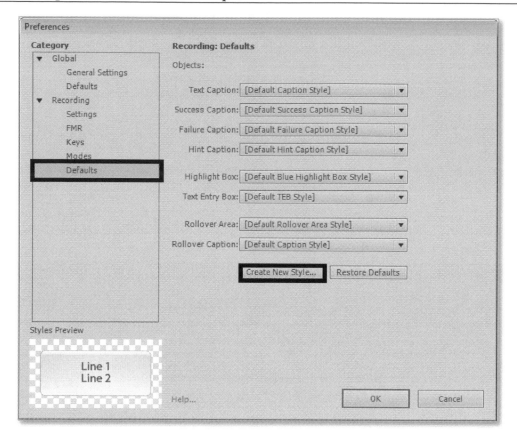

Recording Defaults — Objects Preferences

The Objects Preferences menu allows you to customize the default settings of the automatically generated objects in your recordings. This is particularly useful if you are creating a simulation with highlight boxes and mouse movements, and you would like Captivate to use a particular kind of highlight box or mouse cursor.

Adobe has changed this menu substantially since Captivate 4. You can now set up and save new styles of objects by clicking the **Create New Style** button.

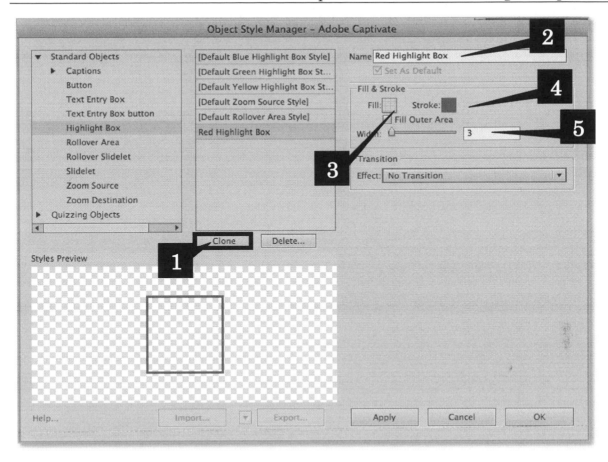

Creating a New Style

You can use the **Object Style Manager** to create and manage new default styles for every kind of object in your project. In this case, we

1. Used the **Clone button** to clone the existing **[Default Blue Highlight box Style]** setting.
2. Gave the style a name.
3. Changed the **Fill** to 0% **Alpha** to reduce its opacity and make it transparent.
4. Changed the **Stroke to red** (#FF0000 in hex). In reality, you should pick a color that fits your clients' needs or your organization's standards.
5. Change the **Width** to 3 pixels.

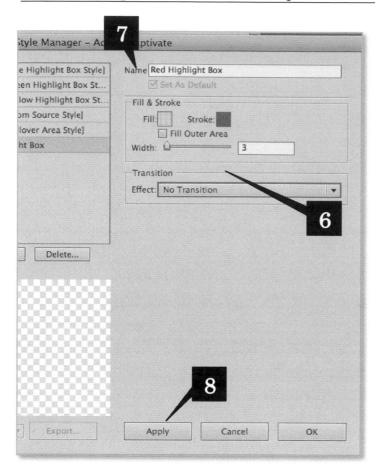

6. Changed the **Transition** option to **No Transition**. (This causes the highlight box to appear suddenly, as opposed to the slow fade-in of a transition. It is better to set this as a default and adjust it on a case-by-case basis in your project)

7. Checked the **Set As Default box**

8. And clicked **Apply**, then **OK**.

You can see that the Red Highlight Box Style now appears in the style menu with the other defaults. You can store multiple defaults in these preferences, and use them in different arrangements that match the rest of your color scheme.

508 Accessibility TIP: Color-impaired Learners

A number of people across the world experience color blindness. If Section 508 compliance is a concern, you can create different kinds of highlight box styles that are easier for colorblind people to see. In the New Style example, a red-green colorblind person might see the Red Highlight box as dark black, much as you see it in black-and-white print.

Red-green colorblind people can see blues and yellows most clearly, so consider those combinations as well. However, a small percentage of people are Yellow-Blue colorblind, so no one color scheme will be perfectly visible to all people. One thing is certain: **to make your objects stand out, avoid pastel colors and lighter-colored transparencies for your various objects.**

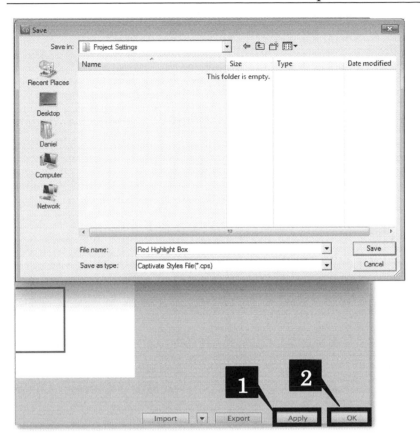

Importing and Exporting an Object Style

If you access the Object Style manager from the **Preferences** menu, you will have the opportunity to save your object style settings for use in future projects. Use the **Export** button to save them as **.CPS** files, and then later use the **Import** button to import those .CPS files into other projects.

Store your style file somewhere safe, and import the file when you create new projects. This will save you a significant amount of time in the long run.

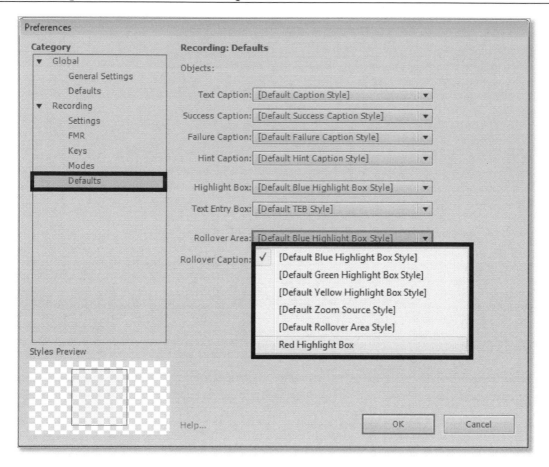

Setting an Object Style as a Recording Default

Here, you can see that the Red Highlight Box style appears in the drop-down menu. We can now select it from the **Highlight Box** menu to apply it as the project default.

Once again, you should determine your project defaults based on existing PowerPoints or promotional materials, your clients' preferences and needs, and your organization's standards.

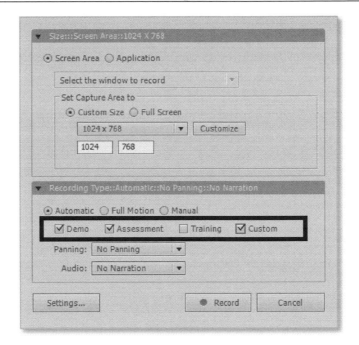

Recording Multiple Project Types

After you adjust the default recording mode settings to your liking, you can check the boxes next to the Recording Type. You can even record all four types of projects by checking all of the boxes at once.

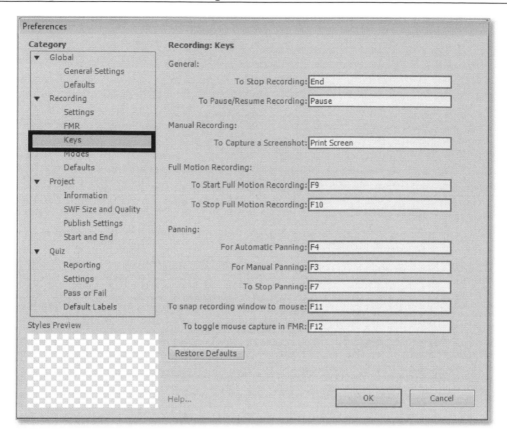

Recording Keys Preferences

Let's take a quick look at the **Recording Keys Preferences screen**, found in the Preferences window, allows you to customize Captivate's hotkeys. You can leave these as defaults, or change the shortcuts to your liking by clicking on the box and entering the new combination.

If you make any changes, make sure that your new hotkeys don't conflict with shortcuts that you might have set for the operating system.

PRO-TIP: Hot Key Conflicts

 If you have more than one screen capture program running at once, make sure that their hotkey settings don't conflict! This is especially important for technical writers who use SnapZ or Jing.

Record, Countdown, and Captivate Icon

Your Captivate project is about to get under way! Now that your settings are all configured, it's time to push the red **Record Button** and get ready for blastoff!

Captivate 5 now features a count-down menu that will give you a few seconds to get yourself ready. This is particularly useful if you are narrating as you record.

1. Once the capture starts, you can stop the capture at any time by pressing **End** key. You can also click the little green Captivate 5 icon at the bottom-left of your screen to end the capture.

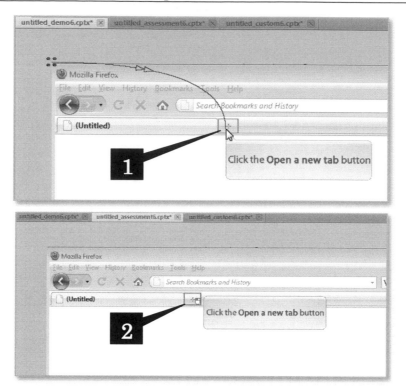

Recording Results: Demo and Assessment

After you end your recording, Captivate will open all of the project types into tabs. In this case, our demonstration and assessment projects appear in two separate tabs.

1. The **Demonstration** at top includes mouse movements, highlight boxes, and text captions (in blue), just as we specified in the options.
2. The **Assessment** below includes click boxes and fail text (in red), but shows no mouse.

As we noted earlier, you can choose to turn the mouse movement on or off at any time.

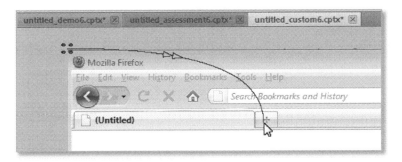

Recording Result: Custom

As we specified earlier, the Custom project adds only the mouse to the screen. We are now free to add highlight boxes and click boxes as we choose. This gives us a much greater degree of flexibility.

 # PRO-TIP: Button Captures

If you notice a number of duplicate captures in your filmstrip, then Captivate is probably taking shots of **Interface buttons**. Interface buttons in programs are usually composed of two images: a button Up state, and a button Down state. The up state is what you first see when you look at a button, and the down state is what you see after you click it. **Captivate will snap screen shots of both states when you click one of these buttons.** This improves the 'realism' of the simulation.

Captivate also automatically sets down state slides to .1 seconds in length, so you can leave the down-state captures alone.

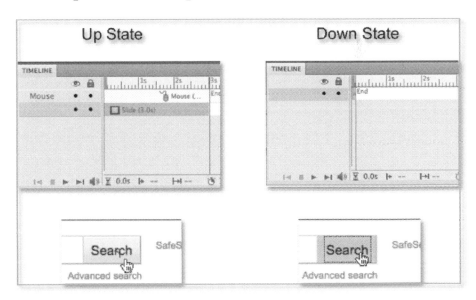

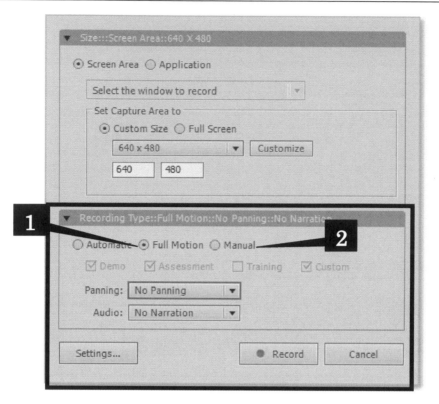

Full Motion Recording and Manual Captures

Now that we've successfully captured some screen shots, we're going to look at the **Recording Type** box. You can use the options in this box to adjust how Captivate will capture your screen shots.

1. If you want to record a smooth, high-resolution, real-time video of a task, or capture a snippet of video from YouTube, you can use the **Full Motion** option. These videos are very large, but very high quality. We recommend that you use this option sparingly. You should also try to delete any unnecessary Full Motion Recordings to reduce your published project's file size.

2. You can also choose the **Manual Recording Mode**. This will prevent Captivate from automatically capturing screenshots. You will need to use your Capture Hotkey to force captures. This is useful if you only need to intermittently capture screenshots in a long process.

Automatic and Manual Panning

Automatic and Manual panning are both achieved through the use of **Full Motion Recording (FMR)**. As we noted earlier, FMR is smooth and pretty, but it increases the file size of your projects and published versions. If your users are on a slow connection, this could cause them some grief. We will discuss FMR more, but you should know that turning off these options could reduce the final size of your final movie at the cost of smoother animated scrolls and drag-and-drops.

In **Automatic Panning** mode, Captivate will follow your mouse around and capture Full Motion video of the specified area around your mouse. This can be useful if you want to show a close-up of a program, or if you want to keep users focused on what you're doing onscreen.

Manual Panning allows you to drag the capture area around the screen. Captivate will record Full Motion video wherever you drop the red rectangle. This is useful for quick overviews of screen areas.

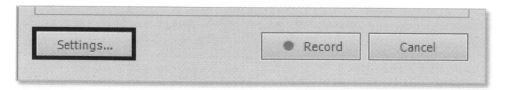

Recording Settings Preferences

Let's return to the **Recording Preferences** by clicking the **Settings...** button.

The Recording Settings window let's you customize a few miscellaneous recording features. The default settings for this menu are generally OK, so you can leave them alone.

However, you might someday need to check or uncheck the boxes under **Automatically use Full Motion Recording for.** When checked, Captivate will use **Full Motion Recording (FMR)** to record your drag-and-drop actions and scrolling in a smooth, movie-like format.

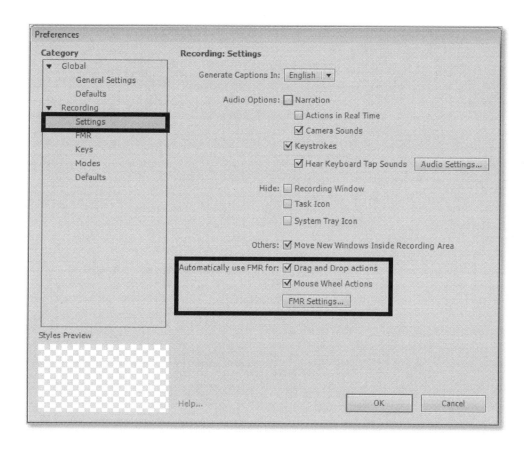

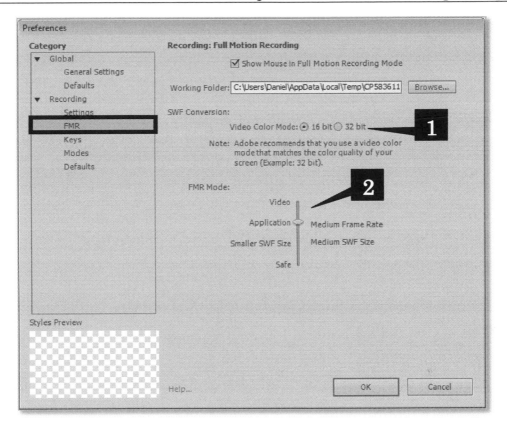

Full Motion Recording Preferences

As we noted earlier, Full Motion Recording is a very useful mode if you have complicated animations to show on the screen. FMR videos record screen actions in real time. This means that it can show changes in mouse buttons, drag-and-drop paths, column reorganizations, and other kinds of animated interface features that Captivate's usual snapshot-based slides can't show as clearly.

We recommend looking at two key options on this screen:

1. **SWF Conversion.** If your learners might be watching these videos on older computers, you might want to change this setting to 16-bit. However, if the learners are on new computers, you might want to choose 32-bit compression.
2. **FMR Mode.** The FMR Mode slider allows you to increase or decrease the quality of the FMR videos in your project. This can help reduce your project's final file size.

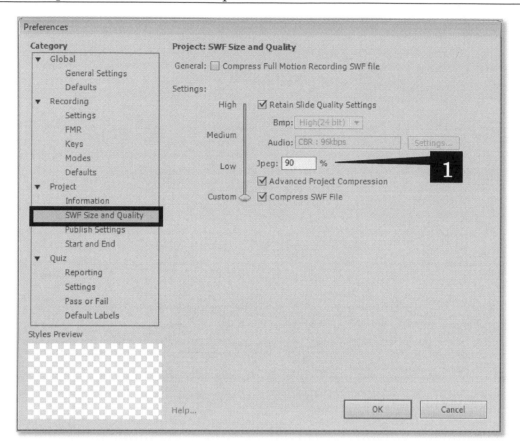

Project SWF Size and Quality Preferences

Let's take this opportunity to look back at the master **Preferences menu** for Captivate, in the **SWF Size and Quality** menu.

1. We recommend leaving the settings alone on this window, but you might want to increase the **JPEG Quality Settings** to 90%.

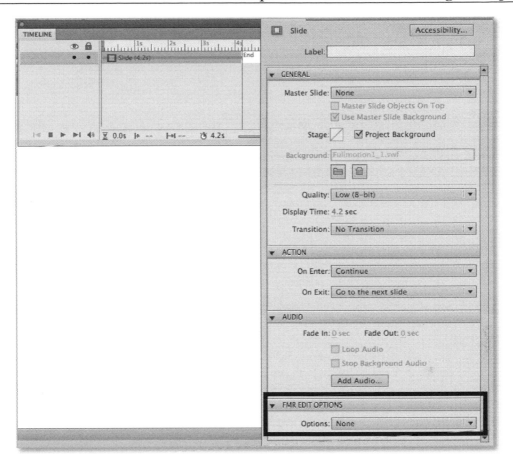

FMR Edit Options Menu

Once you're done recording your Full-Motion project, you'll see your FMR video appear as a new slide in your filmstrip. If you open the timeline for that slide, you'll see that the video is represented as a red line through the slide background row.

The Properties menu for that slide will also contain a new menu: **FMR Edit Options.**

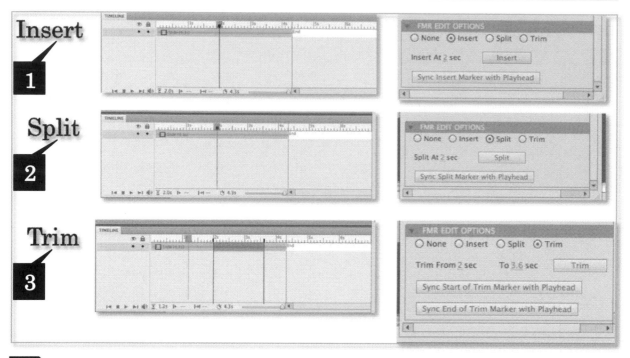

5 NEW: Three Ways to Edit FMRs

The FMR Edit Options menu gives your three choices for editing your Full Motion Recordings:

1. **Insert**. Inserting allows you to place the video into the slide at a particular point in time. This means that you can start a slide with a still image and then later insert the movie into it from the Library. You can drag the small black marker to define the insertion point.
2. **Split**. Split allows you to divide a Captivate file across two or more slides. This is useful if you want to insert a 'freeze-frame' or title slide between two sections of a movie.
3. **Trim**. Trim allows you to drag markers around a FMR to cut sections from the movie. This is useful if an unexpected pop-up appeared during your recording, or if you want to crop out the first few seconds of a video.

Adding Additional Recording Slides

If you want to add a few extra slides into your recording, you can use the Insert > Slide > Recording Slide menu. This will launch the **Record Additional Slides** menu. You can then select the slide that will precede your new slides and start your new capture cycle.

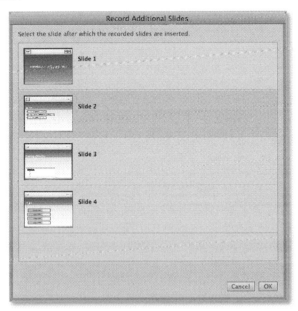

Chapter 4
Objects and
Properties

In this chapter

This chapter will provide you with important information about using objects and properties including:

- Using toolbar objects

- Adding text captions

- Using click boxes for navigation, table of contents, custom quizzes, and closing slides

- Using widgets

- Inserting images and animations

- Using the alignment menu

- Adding Section 508 accessibility to objects and slides

Toolbar Objects

You can insert most of Captivate's objects into your project using the Toolbar. In this chapter, we'll take you through all of the objects you see here, including:

1. Text captions
2. Rollover text captions
3. Highlight boxes
4. Click boxes
5. Buttons
6. Text entry box
7. Rollover slidelet
8. Zoom box
9. Mouse movement
10. Text animation
11. Line tool

Toolbar Options

Before we begin, let's look at some of the non-object options on the toolbar.

12. **Stroke color**. The Stroke color is applied to the line around an object.
13. **Fill Color**. The Fill color is the colorized area inside of an object
14. **Set Stroke/Fill to Black and White**. This changes the Stroke to black and the Fill to white.
15. **Swap Stroke/Fill colors**. This trades the colors and transparencies between the Stroke and Fill boxes.

 PRO-TIP: Merge Object into Background

You can use **cmd-M** to merge an object into the background of a slide. This can be useful if you want to graft images, highlight boxes, or other objects to your slide permanently.

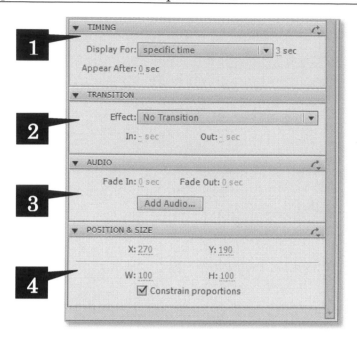

General Object Properties

If you select an object and look at the Properties panel, you'll find that almost all objects in Captivate have the following general properties. We'll discuss them now before we move on to the more complicated object specific settings.

1. **Timing.** The Timing menu allows you to specify when the object will appear or disappear.
2. **Transition.** You can use this option to set the Fade In and Out times, or turn Fade In and Fade Out off completely.
3. **Audio.** You can attach audio to many objects in Captivate through this option, and set the Fade In and Fade Out time.
4. **Position & Size.** If you want to move the object to a specific location on the slide, change the **X and Y values**. If you want to set an object to a specific size, change the **Width (W) and Height (H) values**. The **Constrain proportions** option will keep the objects size in scale.
5. **Apply to All**. You can also use the arrow at the top of each of these sections to apply your settings to all items in your project.

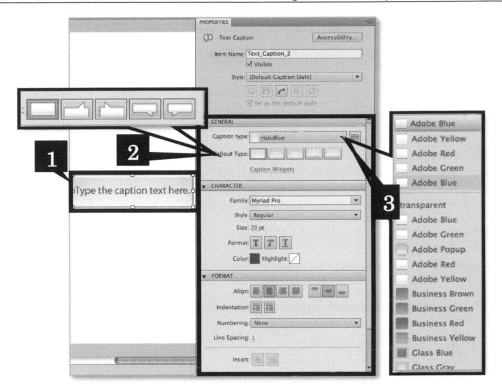

Text Captions

You can use **Text Captions** to describe the actions that are happening in each slide. As we saw in the last chapter, Captivate can automatically generate these when you record your screenshots.

1. You can use the text editing tools in the properties panel to edit the text in the caption.
2. Also, you can use the **Caption Type** menu to change the look and style of your text caption.
3. The Caption Type menu also contains options for changing the orientation and style of the **Caption Outline.**

Captivate includes **Transparent Text Captions**, which you can use to place text onto gradient backgrounds, where a caption box would look conspicuous. See the Shapes section later in the chapter for more information on how to create transparent text captions.

PRO-TIP: Limit Text to Key Words

Don't add too much text to your captions. Instead, use them to highlight key words and phrases from your voiceover.

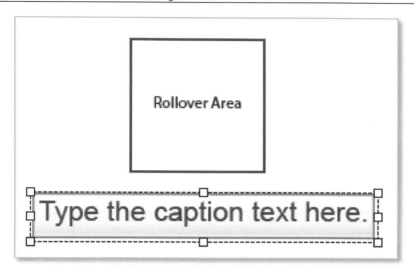

Rollover Text Captions

Rollover Text Captions consist of two parts: a **Rollover Area** and a caption. When a user hovers his or her mouse over the Rollover Area, the caption will appear. Pretty simple.

These objects have a few uses:

1. You can use them to add extra information or help text to your lesson without cluttering the slide.
2. You can use them to annotate detailed diagrams with definitions, directions, or further information without cluttering your slide.
3. You can attach audio to the caption. If you do this correctly, the audio will play when the user hovers over the caption, and stop when they move it. Make sure that the slide audio is over before your Rollover Area appears, or users will hear both audio streams at the same time when they mouse over the area.

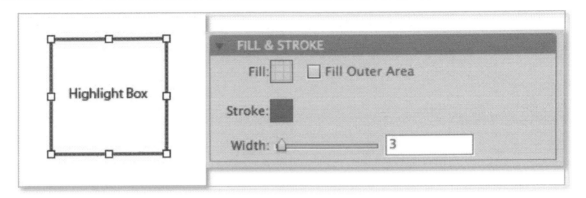

Highlight Boxes

A highlight box is a rectangular object that has two parts: a Fill area and a Stroke line. You can use these boxes to highlight important things onscreen. You can make the Fill area more or less translucent by adjusting the Alpha in the color menu. Remember: An Alpha of 100 is a solid color, and an Alpha of zero is transparent. Anything between those two points is **translucent**.

In this screenshot, you'll see our favorite highlight box. It has a transparent fill, and uses a red (#FF0000 in hex code) stroke of 3. We use this as our default in most projects.

5 NEW: Adjusting Highlight Box Transparency

You can now adjust the transparency of your highlight box's Stroke by clicking on the color menu and reducing the Alpha value.

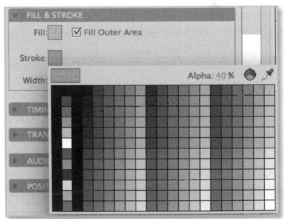

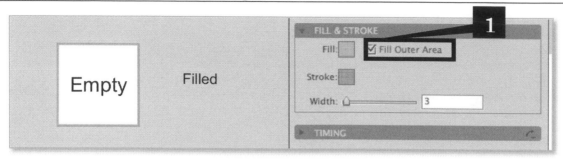

PRO-TIP: Other Uses for Highlight Boxes

You can also create reverse-highlight boxes that

1. Fill the areas outside of the Stroke line by checking the **Fill Outer Area** box. This is useful if you want to call attention to a section of a screenshot, like a menu or window in an interface. You can also place these behind text boxes, so that the text box appears to float on top of a translucent background. Experiment with this feature!

2. You can also use highlight boxes to mask parts of your slide. In this case, we used the **Color Picker (Eyedropper)** to pick up the approximate color of a project's background.

3. Then we placed a filled highlight box over the 'Home button' to mask it on our Index slide. You can then use **Ctrl-M** to flatten the highlight box to the background.

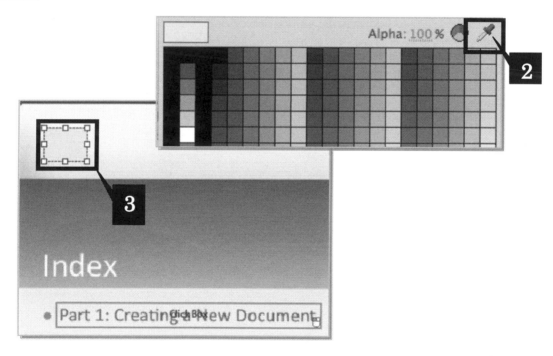

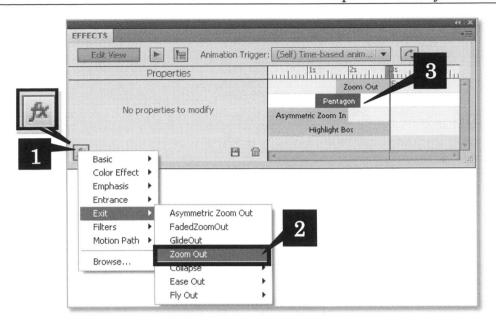

NEW: Motion Effects

Motion Effects are a major new feature in Captivate 5. In essence, Motion Effects are small animation files that allow you to animate your objects. You can apply these small animations to any highlight box, image, or text caption in your project, and control them through the **Effects window**.

1. To add a motion effect to your selected object, you can click the **Add Effect** button in the lower left of the Effects window.
2. Select an effect from the menu.
3. Use the timeline to arrange the order of your effects.
4. You can also adjust some of the effect properties (i.e. the speed, zoom level, etc. of the effect) through the **Effects Properties menu.**

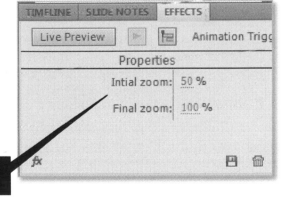

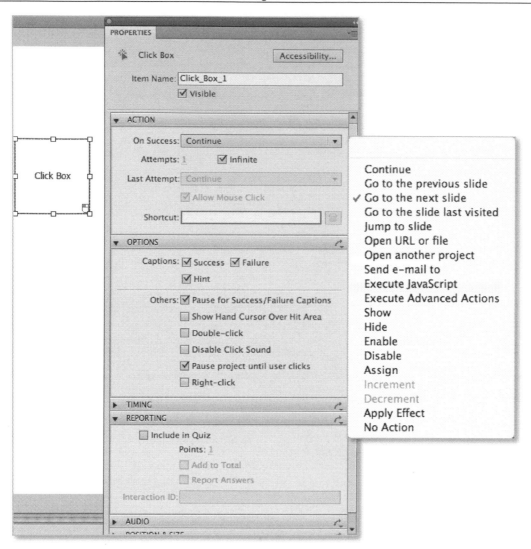

Click Boxes

Click boxes are interactive objects that you can place over top of an area of screen. Users can then click the box to proceed to the next page, send an email, or answer a question.

You can use the **On Success Action** options to create a wide variety of interactive opportunities, as you can see in the screen shot to the right. Also, you can click the **Pause project until user clicks** box to pause projects while users read text or examine images.

Let's take a look at a few practical ways to use these options.

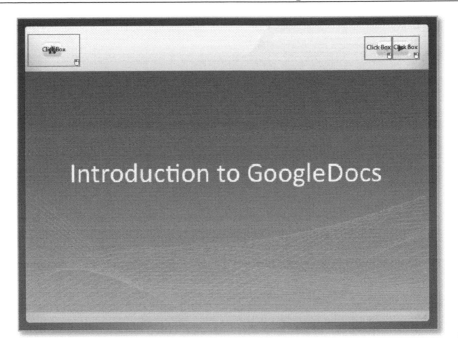

Using Click Boxes for Navigation

You can use click boxes to create simple navigation schemes by setting one click box as **Go to the Previous Slide** and another to **Go to the Next Slide.** We also added a third click box that uses the **Jump to Slide** option to return to slide 1, our home slide. You can then place those click boxes on top of any image or slide element. In this case, we used a PowerPoint template to create our navigation scheme.

 Accessibility TIP: Shortcuts

You can assign a **Shortcut** button to your click box in the properties menu that allows users to control navigation click boxes with keys instead of mice. This is useful for users who might have limited use of their hands.

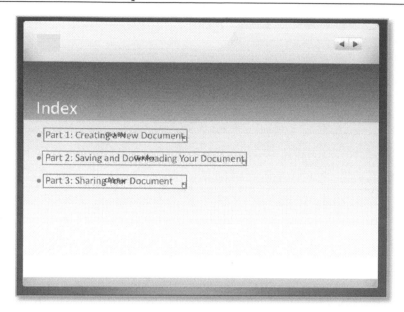

Using Click Boxes in a Custom Table of Contents

You can also use click boxes to create custom indexes for your projects. In this case, we used PowerPoint to create a nice-looking index for our project. When users get to this slide, they can click the title "links" to proceed to those sections.

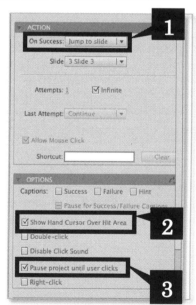

1. The click boxes on top of the titles use the **Jump to Slide** action to jump to their respective parts.
2. We also recommend using the **Show Hand Cursor Over Hit Area** and,
3. **Pause project until user clicks** options in the properties menu to keep the index from advancing before the user is ready. However, if you want the project to **proceed automatically**, you can **uncheck the Pause project option**. Make sure to give the users a few seconds to respond first.

 ## PRO-TIP: Using Click Boxes for a TOC

Using click boxes for a TOC is very useful for performance support-oriented projects. Indexes make it easy for users to find information that is relevant to them. Also, this makes projects more reusable for users who have already seen the module, but are trying to locate specific sections for refresher training.

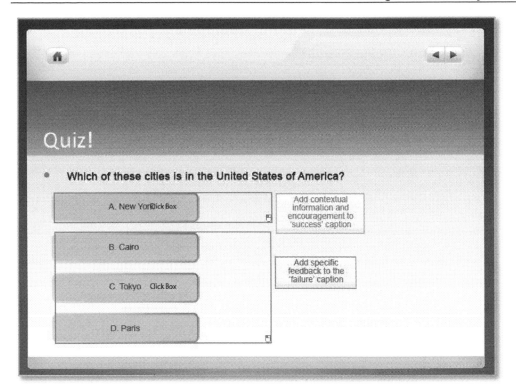

Using Click Boxes in Custom Quizzes

You can also use click boxes to create quick, ad-hoc quizzes for your lessons. Click boxes are always compatible with your templates (unlike Quiz Slides, which need some tweaking).

These **Pop-Quizzes** are very easy to make, and require as few as two click boxes.

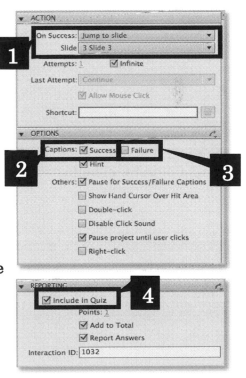

1. Clicking the correct answer sends the user to slide 3 using the **On Success Jump to slide** feature.
2. For the correct answer click box, turn on the **Success Caption**.
3. For the incorrect answers, turn on the **Failure Caption** and do not check the Include in Quiz option.
4. Enable the **Include in Quiz** option in the properties menu.

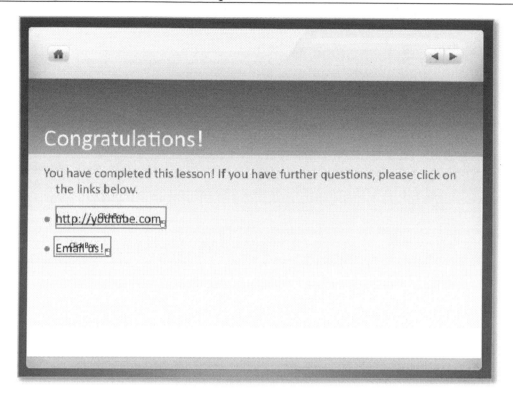

Click Boxes in Closing Slides

We like to use our closing slides to provide extra links and contact information to the user. In this case, we created two click boxes.

1. The first click box opens a link to Google in a new window, where users can search for related videos.

2. The second box opens an email message addressed to a relevant support technician.

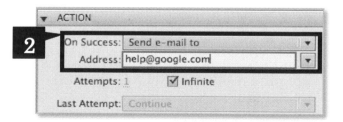

3. In both cases, we recommend you uncheck the **Continue Playing the Project** button.

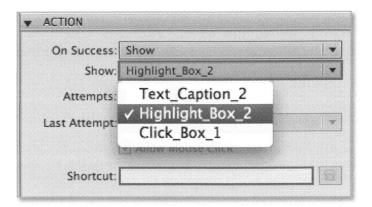

 ## PRO-TIP: Advanced Click Box Features

You can use click boxes to do much, much more than the examples we've shown here. The advanced actions in the **On Success** menu offer you almost unlimited opportunities for creating interactive actions. You can extend the potential of your click boxes using JavaScript, Captivate's Advanced Actions settings, Show, Hide, and Apply Effects.

In this example, we used the **Show** command to reveal a highlight box when the user successfully clicks on the click box.

The Advanced Options are a bit beyond the scope of this book, so we recommend checking blogs and websites for information on how to use these settings. Also, consult with your local Flash guru or the Adobe Forums Captivate community.

 ## PRO-TIP: Click Boxes as Waypoints

You can use click boxes to create waypoints that users must 'touch' as they move through the lesson. They are great for making sure that users are paying attention. Just create an object (caption or shape) with the word "Continue" on it, cover it with a click box, and paste it to your slides. Use these only on key slides. Too many waypoints can annoy learners.

Buttons

Buttons come in three flavors: Text, Transparent, and Image. After adding a button to the slide, you can switch to a different flavor using the **Button Type** drop down menu.

Text Buttons

Text buttons allow you to place interactive buttons with text on the slide. These are fairly simple, and you cannot make any real changes to the button's image. If you'd like to make a more attractive custom button, you can create it as a graphic in Photoshop, and import it onto your slide as an image. Then, you can use the **Make Button Transparent** option to place the transparent text button on top of your image.

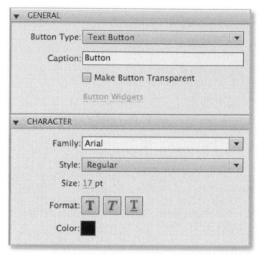

Transparent Buttons

You can also create purely transparent buttons that give you the option to set a Fill and Stroke color. This is basically a hybrid of the click box and the highlight box.

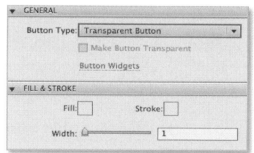

Image Buttons

Captivate 5 includes a whole host of image buttons that you can use in your project. You can also create your own image buttons and add them to the **/Adobe Captivate 5.0/Gallery/Buttons** directory.

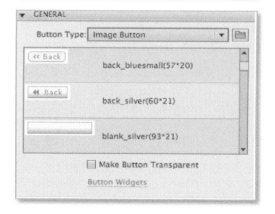

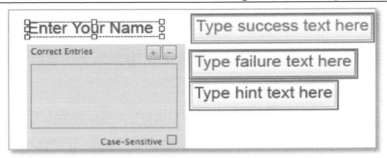

Text Entry Box

Text Entry Boxes are rectangular text entry fields where users can type alphanumeric strings as answers. You can use these boxes to simulate data entry, or you can use them to password protect parts of your training. When you select a text entry box, you are presented with a small panel that allows you to enter the correct answers and turn the **Case-Sensitive** option on or off.

The text entry field has a large array of options, including Actions, Success/Failure/Hint options, and Reporting. You can also Fill the field to make it easier for users to see.

Here are all of the properties available for the text entry box, on one screen:

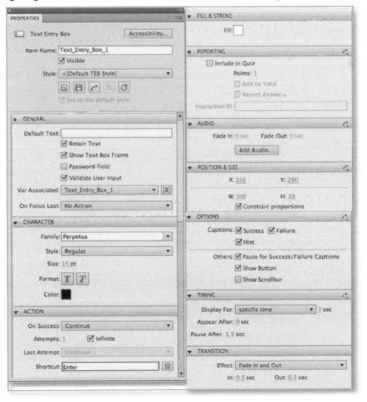

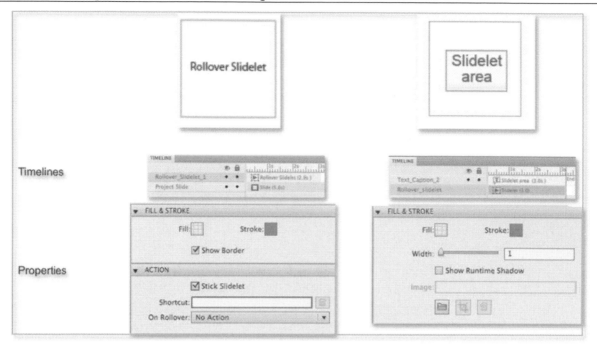

Rollover Slidelets

A **Rollover Slidelet** is a small slide that pops up when the user hovers mouse over the highlight box. The **Rollover Area** is visible on your slide timeline, while the **Slidelet Area** has its own timeline and properties. You can also insert text boxes, rollover text boxes, images, animations, and movies into the Slidelet Area. Any object inserted into a slidelet will only appear on the slidelet timeline.

You can click the **Stick Slidelet** box to leave the slidelet onscreen after users mouse away from the rollover.

You can use slidelets to display detailed maps, add additional movies, and embed extra information into your project without cluttering up the main slide.

However, slidelets can be difficult to use properly. Try to avoid placing too many objects into the slidelet, as the slidelet must be smaller than the rest of the slide. If you overfill it, objects may become too small to see clearly.

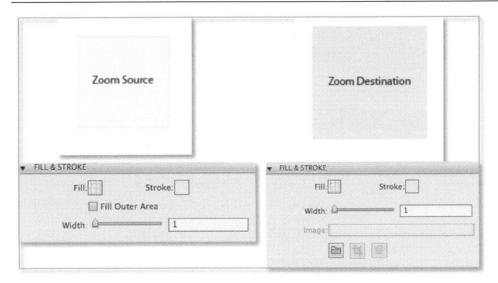

Zoom Boxes

Zoom Boxes are magnifying objects that you can use to highlight very small areas of the screen. They are particularly useful for small buttons and icons, which highlight boxes can obscure.

Just place the **Zoom Source** on top of the part of the screen that you want to magnify. The animation will then show the source expanding until it reaches its full size at the **Zoom Destination**.

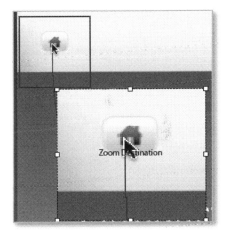

You can also assign an image to the zoom box through the Fill and Stroke properties menu that appears when you select the zoom destination. The destination will then display that image as it zooms out.

You change the amount of time that the zoom box takes to animate by increasing or decreasing the **Zoom for __ sec**. A half-second (.5 sec) zoom is adequate for most situations.

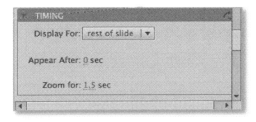

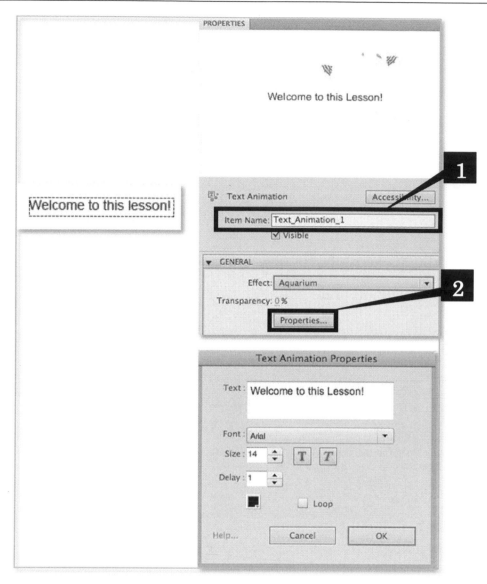

Text Animations

You can add **Text Animations** to your project to draw attention to a title or simulate typing.

1. Use the **Animation Effect** drop down to select an animation style.
2. Click the **Effect Properties** button to open the **Effect Properties menu**. You can enter the text that you want to animate, change the font, style, size, and other details.

 ## PRO-TIP: Use Text Animations Sparingly

Use text animations sparingly, as they can distract and annoy learners.

Typing Text

In addition to the Text Animations that you can add to your project, you'll notice that Captivate automatically creates animations of the text that you enter into websites and applications during your recordings. You cannot edit this **Typing Text** after Captivate records it, so try to get it right the first time.

Captivate records your text entry in real-time, but there's no reason to make a user sit through ten seconds of typing animations. If it took you 15 seconds to type a text string, try shortening it down to three seconds. This will conserve your users' attention spans.

Also, you can use Typing Text to your advantage by synching it up with your audio track and other objects. In the example below, we have shortened our Typing Text so that the animation only occurs during the phrase "Adobe Captivate." This way, users will see the words "Adobe Captivate" typing on screen as they hear the words, thus synching it in their mind.

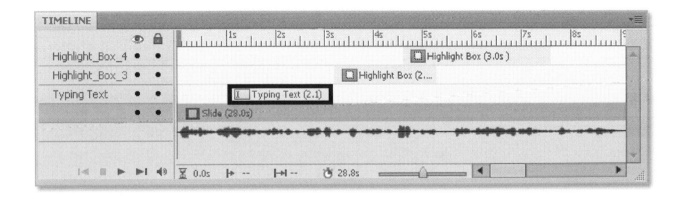

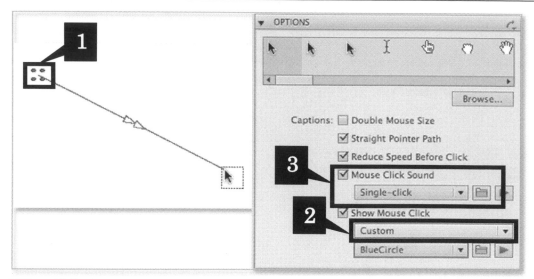

The Mouse

Captivate automatically records the locations of your mouse clicks as your capture your project. When you edit your project, the **Mouse Movement Tool** allows you to reconstruct your mouse's positions through your captures.

1. The first slide of your project that displays a mouse will allow you to place the starting position of the mouse wherever you like by dragging the **Mouse Start Marker**. On every slide after that, the mouse will always start from the previous slide's last position. This can seem strange at first, but you'll get used to it.

In the image above, you can see that we've customized a few options in the mouse properties menu. We recommend using these settings for smooth, attractive mouse movements.

2. You can find several **Custom Mouse Click** animations in the Captivate directory. You can click the directory button next to the drop down menu to see their location.

3. Also, the default Captivate **Mouse Click Sound** leaves a little to be desired. Search online for 'mouse click sounds,' or use a microphone to record a better one yourself!

PRO-TIP: Moving Your Mouse Between Captures

You can move your mouse's position between capture slides by inserting a title slide, image slide or movie. Just activate the mouse on your 'dummy' slide, drag its end point to a new location, and then press delete to hide the mouse. The next slide that has the mouse enabled will start from the title slide's position. This is especially useful if you want to have the mouse travel a longer distance, as this can draw more attention to the area of the screen that you're showing.

Adjusting Mouse Options from the Filmstrip

You can access a number of mouse options from the Filmstrip window. This is useful if you want to select a series of slides and turn them all on at once. You can do this by selecting the slides, right clicking on them, and selecting **Show Mouse** from the menu.

Captivate 5 also allows you to **align the mouse to the previous or next slide** from this menu. Experiment with this option to help keep your mouse actions smooth.

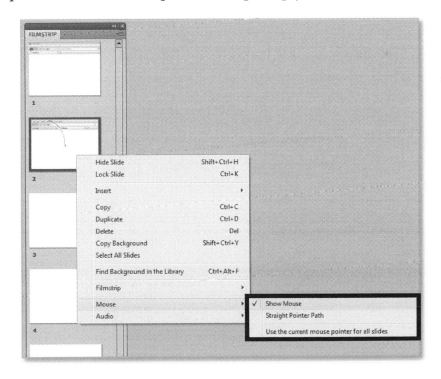

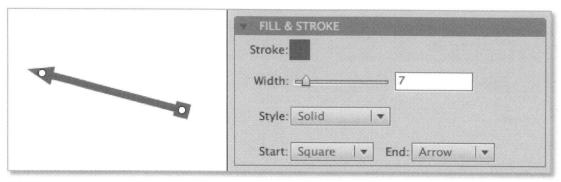

Line Tool

The **Line Tool** allows you to draw custom lines or arrows on your slide. You can adjust the color, width, and style of the arrow, along with the style of the start and end points. You can also attach effects to these objects to animate them.

Other Shapes

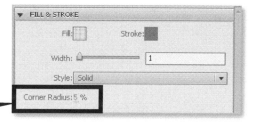

1. If you click and hold your mouse on the Line Tool, you'll notice that a **Rectangle, Oval**, and **Polygon** tool appear in the dropdown menu.
2. In addition to the Fill, Stroke, Width, and Style, you can adjust the **Corner Radius** option on the Rectangle object. This variable allows you to give your rectangles rounded edges. In this case 0% is a 90 degree angle, and 100% turns the rectangle into an oval with straight sides.

Also, Captivate 5 now allows you to add text to your objects (as in PowerPoint). Just double click the object and start typing. You can adjust the font and layout from the Properties window.

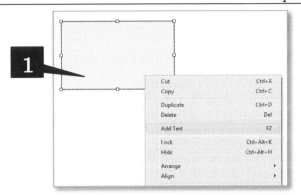

Create Transparent Captions with Shapes

You can also use shapes to create custom semi-transparent captions in multiple colors.

1. The authors recommend creating a standard rectangle or polygon on your stage, then using the **Add Text (F2)** option to add your caption.
2. You can turn the box transparent by reducing the Shape's Fill Alpha to 0, and the Width to 0, as you see in, or leave it slightly filled-in with a color of your choosing.

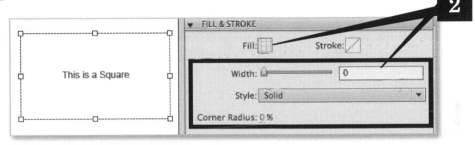

In the image below, we have developed a nice quiz template in PowerPoint. All we have to do is add transparent squares with captions, and our quiz is ready to use!

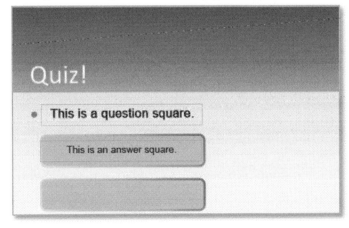

Widgets

Widgets are very powerful and complicated SWF files that can perform specific functions. This topic is a little beyond the scope of this book, but we recommend visiting blogs and YouTube to find out more. You'll also find a section on Widgets in the Captivate 5 User Guide, as well as the Adobe Help menu. Try searching the Internet for the Twitter and GoogleMaps widgets to get a sense of what these mini-applications can accomplish.

1. In this case, we've inserted a basic **Certificate of Course Completion** widget into a project from the Widget window. This particular widget prints out a certificate of completion that can be provided to your human resources department.
2. As the widget loads, you will be able set a number of preferences.
3. When you've entered all of your parameters, the Certificate widget will appear onstage, ready for use.

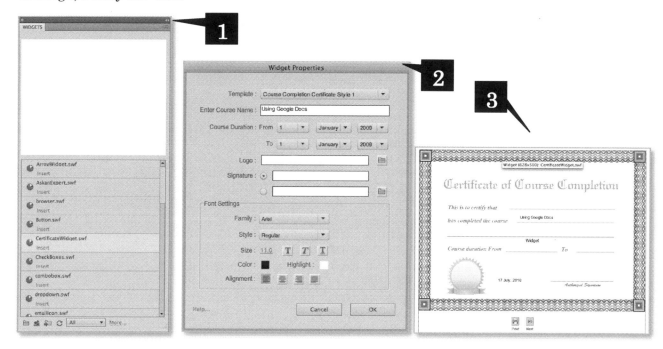

5 NEW: Enhanced Widgets

Captivate 5 includes additional and higher quality prebuilt widgets, playbars, skins, animations, images, text captions, and buttons with improved usability.

Inserting Images

In addition to the objects, you can also import a wide variety of image formats into your slides. You should choose the format that best preserves the quality of your images. Let's look at the relative strengths of each format:

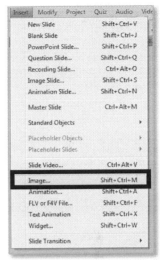

- **JPG** – Small file size, but the compression causes the image to get fuzzy around the edges of lines. Useful for most photographs.
- **PNG** - Small file size, good compression, crisp lines, transparency layers. You can use this for most images.
- **GIF** – Crisp edges and transparency layers, but fewer colors. Useful for simple images such as logos.
- **BMP** – Large file sizes, but high quality images. These can bloat the size of your Captivate library.
- **PSD** – Photoshop Document, very large file sizes, but you can edit all of the layers in the image in Photoshop.

Be sure to scrub any passwords or sensitive information from your images in Photoshop before you publish your project. If you don't have Photoshop, cover sensitive information with Shapes or Highlight boxes.

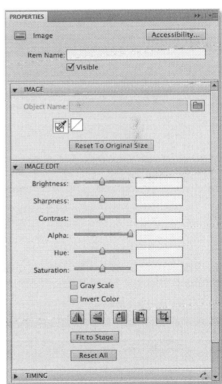

Once you have imported your image, you can use the Properties menu to adjust a number of the image's properties. These include the Brightness, Sharpness, Contrast, Transparency, Hue, and Saturation. You can also change the image to grayscale, invert the color, flip it, rotate it, and crop it.

Captivate has a number of new features that allow you to work with your PSD files without leaving the program. After importing a PSD, look for the Photoshop icon on your screen. Clicking the icon will activate Photoshop. When you are done, Captivate will load the new version of the PSD into your project.

Insert Animations

You can use the **Insert Animations** option to add pre-made and custom SWF and GIF animation files to your project. In rare instances, an inserted Flash SWF may not display correctly, perhaps because of _root layer issues ((consult your Flash developer).

Adobe has included a number of animated files that you can add to your project. You'll find them in the **/Adobe Captivate 5/Gallery/SWF Animation** directory. You can use them to spruce up your slides.

You can also adjust the timing and transparency of the SWF through the Properties menu. You can view the **animation information** by pressing the information icon.

The Alignment Menu

Keep in mind that good graphic and visual design must exhibit four essential qualities to varying degrees: **Contrast**, **Alignment**, **Repetition,** and **Proximity (CARP)**. Good alignment goes a long way towards helping you achieve high-quality visuals.

Once you have added your objects to the timeline, you might want to use the **Alignment Menu** to crisply align your objects. We highly recommend that you use these options to keep you object in a tidy visual relationship.

PRO-TIP: Ctrl-Z (Undo)

You should become familiar with **Ctrl-Z** (the undo command) as you work on the alignment of your projects. It is often much quicker and easier to simply undo your last error than to try to fix it.

508 Accessibility TIP: Adding Accessibility to Objects

You can add 508-compatible accesibility text to any object in your project by selecting the object and clicking the **Accesibility** button.

By default, the **Auto Label** button will be checked. You can uncheck the box and enter an Accessibility name and description that can help the vision imparied 'see' what's going on in your movie through their screen readers.

508 Accessibility TIP: Adding Accessibility to Slides

You can also add 508 accessibility to your slides, by selecting the slide, clicking on the Accesibility button in the Properties menu, and clicking the **Import Slide Notes** button in the **Slide Accesibility** menu.

Chapter 5
Audio Recording and Editing

In this chapter

This chapter will provide you audio and recording information including:

- Recording from the slide

- Importing audio

- Using text to speech

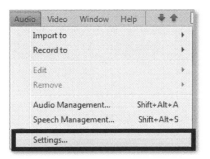

Configuring Your Audio Settings

Before you start recording voice narration for your project, you should adjust the **Audio Settings**. You can find the Audio Settings menu throughout the Captivate 5 interface, but you can always activate it from the Audio menu.

There are three main options for you to adjust in this menu:

1. **Audio Input Devices**. You can use this drop-down to select your recording device. If you're using a USB headset to record, make sure you select it from this drop down.
2. **Bitrate.** Under certain circumstances, **Variable Bitrate (VBR)** recordings can yield smaller files, but **Constant Bitrate** is generally less processor intensive. We recommend using Constant Bitrate to minimize the chance of audio artifacts and skipping audio. Also, we recommend using a bitrate of 64kbps if your users are watching the video over the Internet. If you are publishing to a disk or LAN, you can use a higher bitrate like 96kbps.
3. **Calibrate Input**…Try to remember to use the Calibrate Input tool every time you record in a new room. Adjusting the levels can help you get better sound. You can also use it to make sure that your microphone is on and not muted, and that your recording level is high enough.

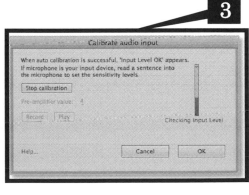

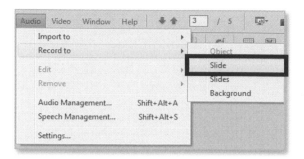

Recording Audio to a Slide

Once your Audio settings are configured, you can use the **Record to | Slide** to open the **Slide Audio** window. We'll return to this window several times in this chapter, but for now, we have three concerns

1. The **Record** button.
2. The **Preview** button. You can use this button to preview your slide animations, or narrate an FMR.
3. The **Captions & Slide Notes** button. Use this to bring up the script you typed into your slide notes.

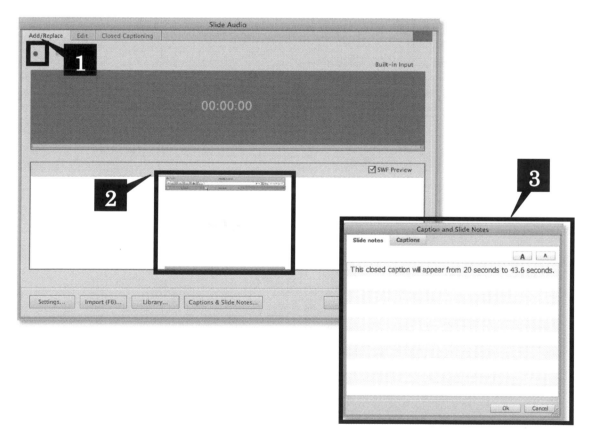

Time to Record!

You've pressed the Record button and the countdown has begun! Soon, you'll be immortalizing your content, bit by bit!

 ## PRO-TIP: Better Voiceovers

You can do a few things to improve the quality of your voiceover narration.

- Sit up straight in your chair.
- Breathe from your diaphragm.
- Keep some water handy, but avoid teas, milk, and soda for at least an hour before you start.
- Some people recommend standing up during audio recording. This keeps your body more upright and your chest more expanded than sitting.
- Try to record all of your audio during the same time of day, either morning or afternoon. Peoples' voices change in pitch and volume throughout the day, so try to stay consistent.
- **Smile while you narrate.** The human brain can detect very small shifts in vocal expression. Your users will hear the subtle ways in which your speech changes through a smile, and it will put them at ease.

When you're done narrating, press the Stop button to end the recording. Captivate will then display the audio as a waveform.

Click the Save button, then close the window using the Close button.

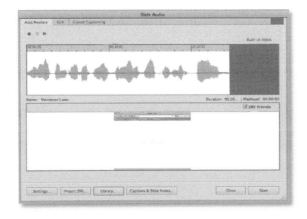

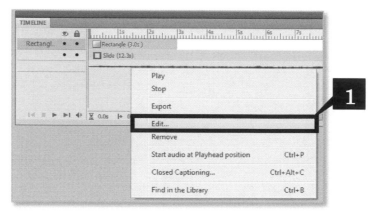

Editing Slide Audio

1. You can access the audio editing panel by right clicking on the audio in the Timeline and selecting and selecting **Edit**.
2. This will open the **Slide Audio Edit Tab**. You can use this window to listen to your audio and delete selected portions of it. We recommend that you use the space bar to play and pause the audio. You can use this menu to cut, copy, paste, and delete any portion of your audio. You can also use the slider to zoom in and out on the waveform.

When you come to a patch that you would like to delete, select it and press the delete key.

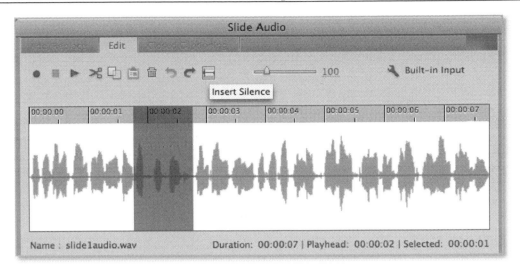

Inserting Silence

The **Insert Silence** button allows you to add silence between sections of your audio, or edit audio out of your file by selecting an area and 'filling' it with silence.

If your narration includes lists or sequences, you can use the button to emphasize key words by adding pauses around them, or, you can use the Insert Silence button to blank segments of your audio.

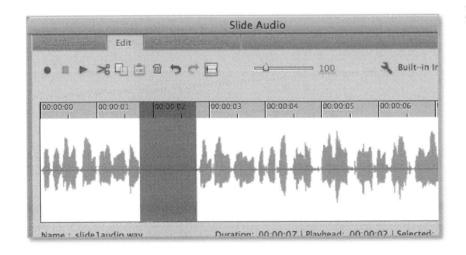

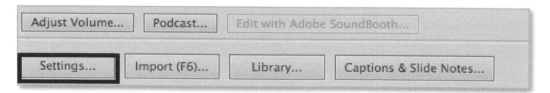

The Adjust Volume Menu

You can click the **Adjust Volume** button at the bottom of the Slide Audio window to bring up the Adjust Volume window. You can change two key variables in this menu.

 PRO-TIP: Volume Settings

1. **Volume.** If you find that your recording is too low to hear properly, you can try increasing the volume using this slider. Otherwise, **we recommend that you decrease your volume to -3 dB.** This will help prevent audio problems when you normalize your audio.

2. **Audio Processing. For this option, we recommend that you select Normalize.** Normalizing your audio will average out the sound wave peaks to create a smoother volume level. If your narration has loud parts and quiet parts, you can use the **Dynamics** option and sliders to smooth out the volume within a particular range.

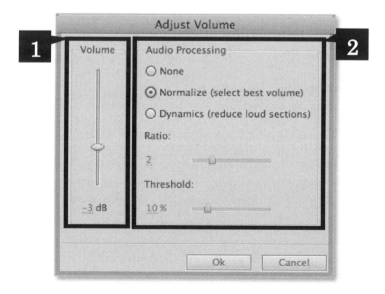

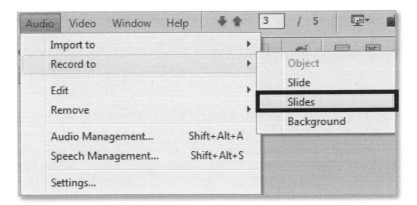

Recording Audio Across Multiple Slides

Sometimes, you may need to spread your audio over several slides. This frequently happens when creating software demonstrations of programs that have many drop down menus. You can use the **Record to | Slides** window to break your audio out across several slides. Just drag the dark lines to the right positions, and click the Save button at the bottom of the window. Captivate will then place each section onto its proper slide.

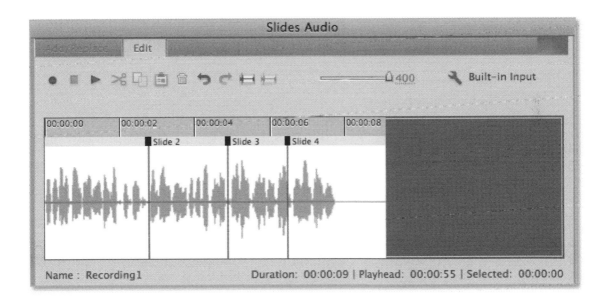

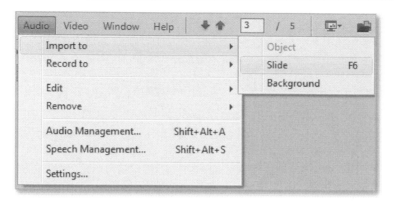

Importing Audio to a Slide

If you have recorded your audio in a different program (i.e. Adobe Soundbooth, GarageBand, or Audacity), you can select a slide from the Filmstrip and use the **Import to Slide** feature to bring those WAVs or MP3s into your project.

 PRO-TIP: Dragging and Dropping Audio Files

You don't always have to use the import menu. You can drag and drop your audio files directly from your Windows folder onto your slides. You can also use the **Import... button in the Library Window** to import all of your audio to the Library at once. You can then drag and drop them from your Library onto the slide icons in the Filmstrip.

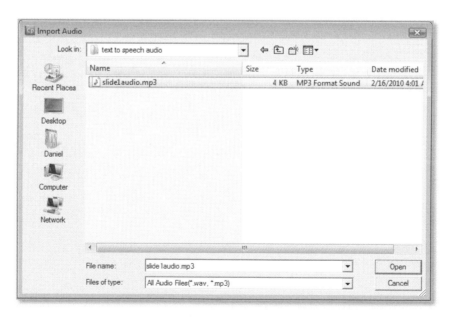

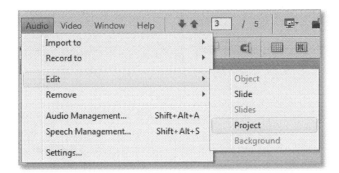

Editing Project Audio

If you imported a pre-recorded audio track to a slide, you can use the **Edit | Project** menu option to divide the audio across the project's slides. Just drag the slide markers to your desired position and Captivate will automatically divide the audio files across those slides.

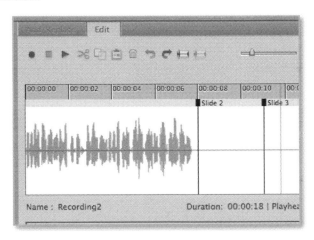

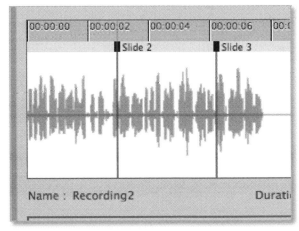

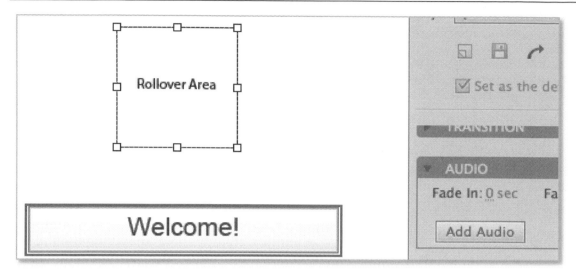

Inserting Audio onto an Object

You can attach audio to an object using the **Add Audio** button in the **Properties** menu. In this example, we've added audio to an invisible rollover area so that the audio will only play if the user hovers over the "Welcome" box. This is useful if you are doing language training, performance support, or software for children.

Make sure that your rollover boxes do not appear until after your slide audio has finished.

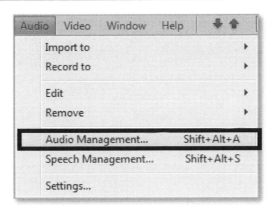

The Audio Management Menu

You can use the **Audio Management** window to see the audio files that are attached to your slides. This is very useful if you want to make sure that each slide has its appropriate audio. This menu will also tell you the audio duration, size, original file name, audio sampling rate, and bitrate.

In this example, we've checked the **Show object level audio** box, which also shows us objects that have audio attached to them. In this case, we have a rollover area in slide 1 that has a 7.7 second audio file attached to it.

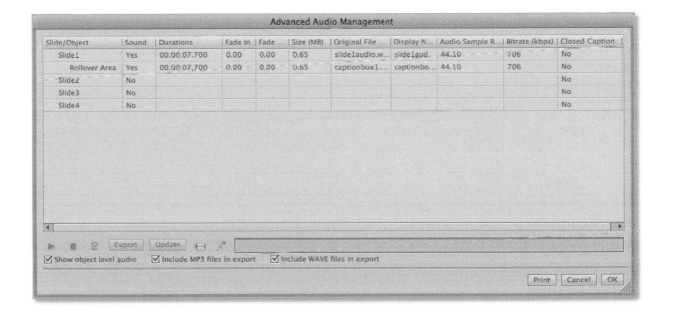

PRO-TIP: USB Microphone Headsets

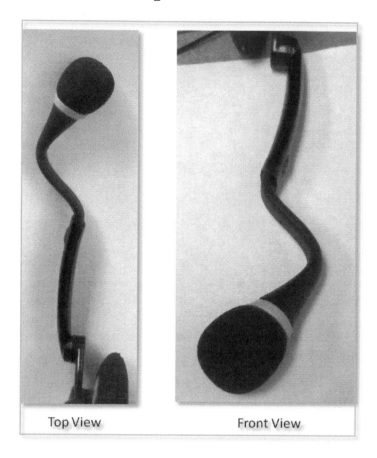

Top View   Front View

If you're serious about recording narration for your Captivate project (and you should be), we recommend the **Plantronics Audio 470 USB Headset**. You can find it on Amazon.com or at your local computer store for less than $50. This headset is comfortable to wear and compatible with your PC via the included USB dongle.

(DO NOT accidentally throw away the USB dongle. It provides better recording quality than plugging directly into a Microphone port.)

We also recommend that you bend the **Microphone Boom** (the flexible part that comes from the left side of the headphones) into a zig-zag shape, as shown above. This will help you avoid annoying pops and clicks that appear when your inhalation and exhalations are picked up by the microphone.

Chapter 6
Video

In this chapter

This chapter will provide you with important information for working with videos including:

- Inserting Video Files

- Using the Adobe Media Encoder for Mobile Devices

- Understanding the Video on the Timeline

- Editing Video Timing

- Using the Video Management Menu

- Inserting an FLV or F4V

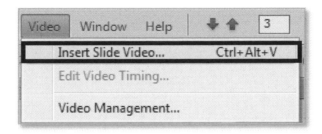

Inserting Video Files

Captivate 5 now accepts a wide variety of video files. Whether you are shooting your video with a high-end digital video camera, a cheap point-and-shoot, or using a webcam, you should be able to import it into Captivate.

You can import your video by clicking the **Video** menu at the top of the screen, and selecting **Insert Slide Video**. You'll find that you can import the following formats:

- **FLV/F4V** – Flash Live Video, useful for movies with a lot of motion
- **AVI** – Audio-Video Interleave, a wrapper package that contains a video file and an audio file.
- **MP4** – A small, portable video format that encodes video using the H.264 video codec and mp3 audio. You'll find it used by most portable devices these days, including iPods and Flip products.
- **MOV** – Apple's proprietary QuickTime video format. It provides very crisp Full Motion Recording videos.
- **3GP** – A video format common to mobile phones that don't use MP4.

Please note that Captivate will automatically encode all of these formats to FLV when you import them. This can take some time, so be sure to budget accordingly.

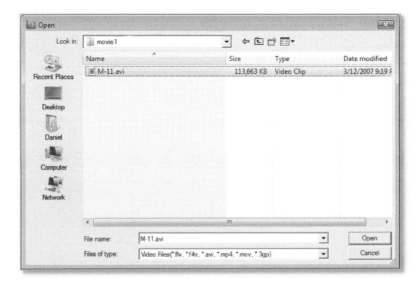

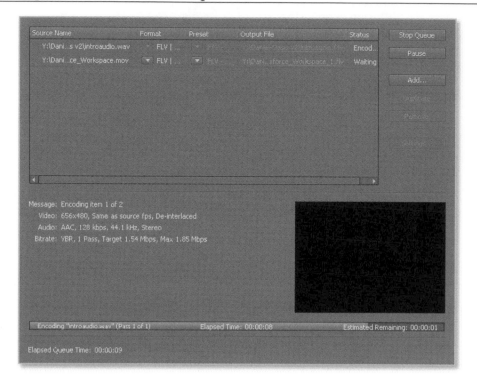

Adobe Media Encoder (AME)

When you install Captivate, the installer will also include a program called **Adobe Media Encoder**. This program is extremely useful, because you can use it to convert almost any movie format (except SWF) into FLV. Captivate will automatically open the AME whenever you import a non-FLV video file.

However, you can also use the AME to convert your videos to Captivate-ready files without importing them individually into Captivate. Start by opening the AME. Then, drag and drop your media files directly into the AME. Once you drop them, the AME will start to queue your files into a batch. It will then begin a 2-minute countdown to Queue encoding, unless you kick-off the conversion early by pressing the **Start Queue** button.

Message: Queue encoding will start in 1 min 53 sec or press Start Queue to start now.
Video:
Audio:
Bitrate:

Adobe Media Encoder for Mobile Devices

You can also change the output settings of your movie files by clicking on the **Settings...** option in the AME interface.

There are some very advanced **Export Settings** here, we'll take a look at an interesting feature is the ability to change the **Export Format** to H.264. This will let you convert your files into a format that works on mobile devices.

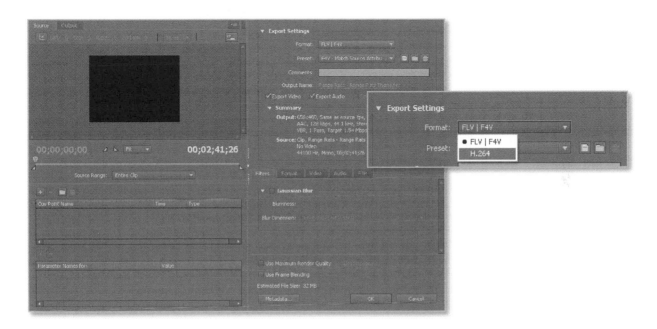

Video on the Timeline

Once your video has been encoded to FLV, it will appear on your timeline. You can then choose when it will appear, and whether it will fade in and out.

Captivate 5 will also allow you to **apply motion effects to your videos**. This way, you can use the more advanced cuts and fades to transition between your still captures and video files. Experiment with this feature to find new ways to use it!

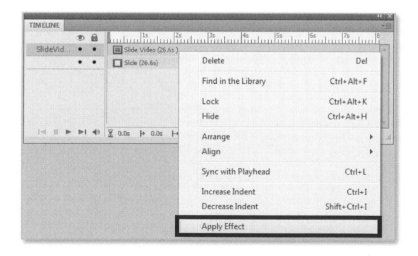

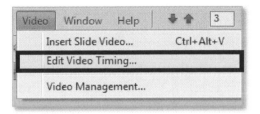

Editing Video Timing

You can access the **Edit Video Timing** option from the Video menu or through the Properties menu. The Edit Video Timing window allows you to split your video clips across several slides. This is useful if you want to start each part of your video with a still title card. You can drag the slide markers left and right to change the timing, and use the **Slide Preview mode** to see how the video will look after it is divided across the slides.

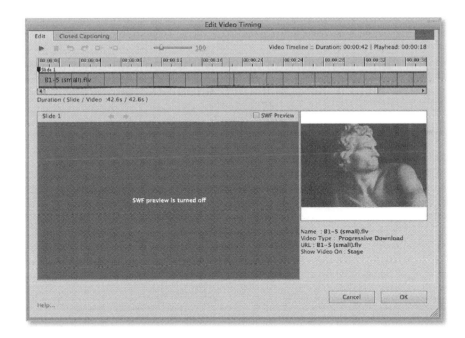

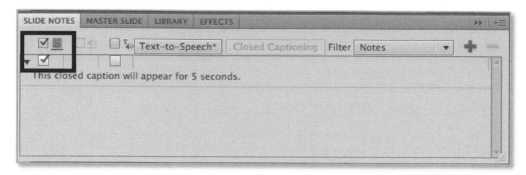

508 Accessibility TIP: Closed Captioning Your Video

You can also add closed captions to your videos by checking the **Video CC** box in the Slide Notes window. This will automatically make your slide notes available through the Edit Video Timing menu's Closed Captioning tab. In this tab, you can choose when you would like the slide notes to appear by dragging the corresponding markers left and right.

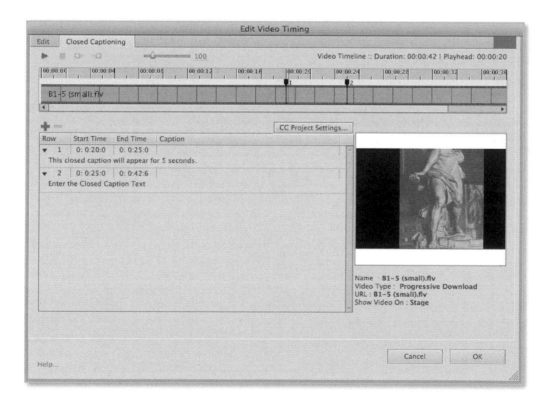

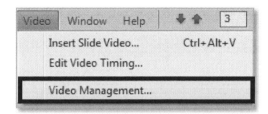

The Video Management Menu

You can also access the **Video Management** window from the Video drop down menu. The Video Management menu tells you where all of your project's videos are located, what type of video they are, and whether the videos are visible from the Stage or Table of contents. This is useful for keeping track of your video settings and placements.

You can also use the **Show Video On** drop down to select whether your movie will appear in the project's Table of Contents, which you can publish later.

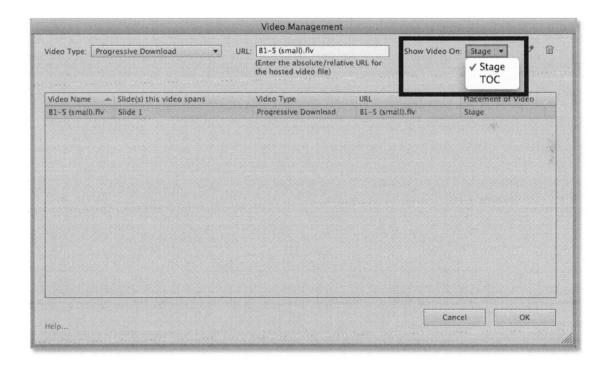

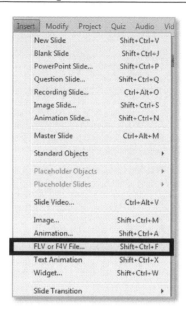

Insert an FLV or F4V

If you already have a video in FLV or F4V format, you can use the **Insert | FLV or F4V File...** to import the video to your slide.

When you select that option, the **Import Video** menu will appear. You can then select a video file from your computer by selecting the **On your Computer** radio button and browsing for the file.

Unless you have a web server that can stream flash videos, do not select the **Already deployed to a web server option**.

FLV or F4V Properties

Once your FLV file appears on the slide, you can use the properties window to view a few options. You can choose from three **Video Types: Progressive Download**, **Streaming Video**, and **Flash Video Streaming Service.** Unless you have a good reason to change it, set the type to Progressive Download.

You can also change the FLV's playbar look by selecting a new skin from the **Skin** drop-down menu.

Chapter 7
Slide Notes, Text-to-Speech, and Closed Captions

In this chapter

This chapter will provide you with all the information you will need to set up text to speech and closed captioning with Adobe Captivate 5 including:

- Understanding the Slide Notes Window
- Enabling Text-to-Speech
- Using the Speech Management Window
- Understanding Closed Caption Timing
- Publishing Your Closed Captions

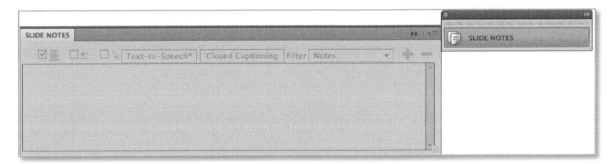

The Slide Notes Window

The **Slide Notes Window** will be useful to you at a number of points during your project. At its most basic level, the Slide Notes window is a place to store anything that you might want to remember about your slides. You can store notes to yourself, notes to developers, or ideas about things that you want to do later.

But the Slide Notes window does much more than that. We recommend that you type your voiceover script directly into the Slide Notes window after you record your slides. This will help you keep your narration clear and concise.

You can use the plus sign at the top right of the window to **Add a new slide note**, and the minus sign to remove one. We recommend that you use these text entry areas to group your notes. You don't have to put each sentence in its own box, but try to group them in a natural and logical order. If you want to rearrange your notes, you can click and drag them up and down the list.

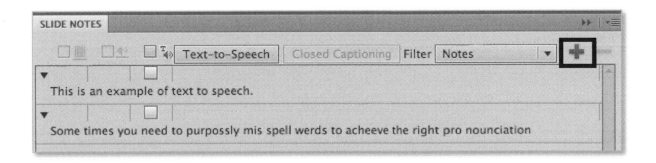

Enabling Text-to-Speech

Text-to-Speech (TTS) is one of the most useful features in Captivate 5. If you have captured your slides and entered your script into the Slide Notes field, you can use TTS to immediately add audio narration to your project.

Text-to-Speech will help you put together a quick prototype that you can show to learners and clients for feedback. The computerized voices are not ideal for finished narration, but they will allow you to assess your project as you go.

To get your Slide Notes ready for Text-to-Speech, check the **TTS** box at the top left of the window. This will check all of your slide notes as being part of your TTS audio narration. Then, press the **Text-to-Speech** button to open the Speech management window.

If you see **Text-to-Speech*** (with an asterisk) displayed on your TTS button, Captivate is alerting you that you have made changes to your Slide Notes but not yet generated new TTS audio. You must regenerate your audio every time you make changes to your script.

 ## NEW: Text-to-Speech Voices in Captivate 5

Adobe provides three new voices in Captivate 5. See the Speech Management section for more information.

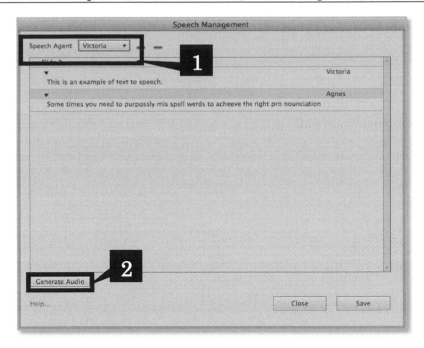

The Speech Management Window

The **Speech Management** window will convert your slide notes to Text-to-Speech audio.

1. This window lets you choose a **Text-to-Speech Agent** from the drop down menu at the top.
2. Then, press the **Generate Audio** button.

Captivate 5 is configured to discover and load all of the Text-to-Speech voices that exist on your system. You will see the text-to-speech agents that Microsoft has included with Windows.

Adobe also provides five voices. For example, Kate and Paul from NeoSpeech (American English) are good, solid choices for your project. They speak at a reasonable pace, and are easy to understand.

Adobe has also included British, French, and German TTS agents from Loquendo. You can use these voices, along with others, to localize the training for a specific user population. You should install both the NeoSpeech and Loquendo voices when you first install Captivate 5.

If a word doesn't sound right when your TTS agent speaks it, try an alternative or phonetic spelling. This occurs most frequently when a noun and verb are spelled the same but pronounced differently (as in 'create a project' and 'project a slide').

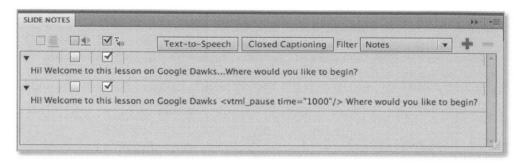

 PRO-TIP: Making Your TTS More Expressive

Text-to-Speech engines are actually very complicated algorithms that synthesize the syllables in written text into audio phonemes. Our brains have no trouble understanding those synthesized words, but the lack of emotion in the voice can make it difficult for a person to connect emotionally with the information.

We recommend that you use punctuation to improve the timing and expressiveness of the synthetic voices. For example, you can use ellipses to add pauses between list items, and question marks after questions.

If you're feeling confident, you can use the **Voice Text Markup Language (VTML)** to directly communicate with the Text-to-Speech engine in Captivate. Look for guides to this language online, and you can make very specific changes to the pitch, intonation, and accent marks in your text. Search for Voice Text Markup Language online, and you'll find several guides to working with it online.

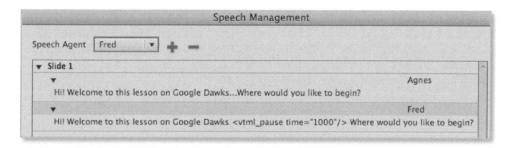

 PRO-TIP: Virtual Conversations

If you want to create a 'conversation' between virtual 'people', you can select a slide note and choose a new voice from the drop down. That voice will only 'speak' its assigned lines. This is especially useful if you want to dramatize a historical event, perform a mock interview, or tell an instructional narrative.

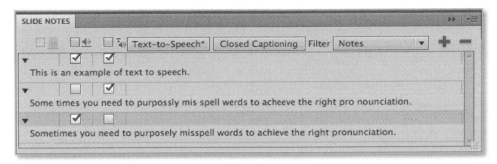

Accessibility TIP: Configuring Your Closed Captions

In addition to housing your script and creating your Text-to-Speech audio, the Slide Notes menu can manage your **Closed Captioning**. Closed Captions are very useful to older and hearing-impaired users who might not be able to hear your audio narration.

As we mentioned earlier, you may find that you need to use alternate or phonetic spellings of words to make them sound correct. If you used these spellings as closed captions the text might confuse or distract your users. To keep your closed captions pristine, create a new slide note with the correct spelling. Leave your note's Text-to-Speech box unchecked, and check the **Audio Closed Captioning** box. When your project publishes, Captivate will automatically add the closed captions.

Closed Caption Timing

You can click the **Closed Captioning** button in the slide notes menu to edit your caption timing. You can then use the black sliders to indicate when you want the caption to appear.

You can also click the **CC Project Settings** to increase or decrease the **Lines** (number of caption lines that appear onscreen at once) and the background color of the caption display area.

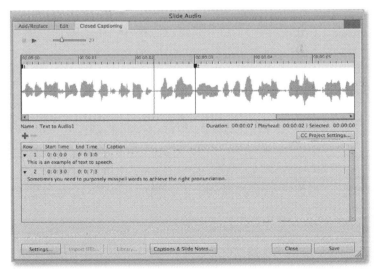

Publishing Your Closed Captions

In order to make your Closed Captions available to your users, you'll need to check the Closed Captioning box in the Skin Editor menu. This will add a **CC** button to the playbar that users can use to toggle closed captions on and off.

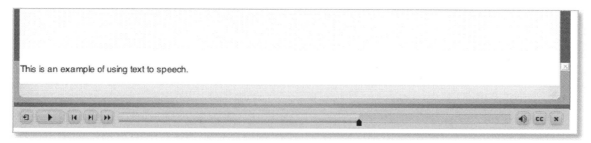

This is an example of using text to speech.

Accessibility TIP: Giving Users Control of Closed Captions

To use projects created in Captivate on the Web, many people who are deaf depend on captions for audio content. Make sure the skin has the closed caption and volume control options enabled so the use can control whether they see closed caption or are able to adjust the volume.

Chapter 8
PowerPoint, Templates, and Master Slides

In this chapter

This chapter will provide you with what you need to work with PowerPoint, templates, and master slides including:

- Starting With PowerPoint
- Creating a New Project Template
- Preparing Reusable Slides
- Working with Custom Master Quiz Slides
- Creating Slide Groups
- Using the Template

Starting With PowerPoint

Unless you are a skilled graphic designer, we recommend that you begin your template design with Microsoft PowerPoint 2007 or 2010. This version of PowerPoint contains some excellent templates, objects, graphics, and clip art.

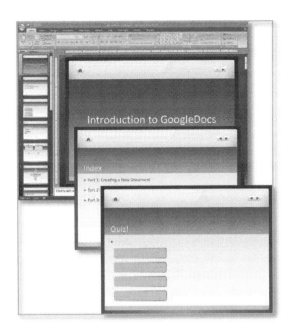

In this example, we have created a series of slides in PowerPoint that will function as template components in Captivate. We'll navigate to the File menu in PowerPoint and click the **Save as Pictures** function. This will lead us to the export screen.

 ## PRO-TIP: PowerPoint

1. Use PowerPoint to combine several graphics on a slide into one using the Grouping function. Then, you can use the right-click menu to save these as PNGs. You can then import them to Captivate.
2. Copy and paste images and graphics directly from PowerPoint to Captivate. These copy/pasted objects will be added to your library.
3. Check out PowerPoint's excellent drawing and clip art tools. Need a picture of a ringing clock? You'll find one in the clip art gallery.
4. Look for more high-quality PowerPoint templates on Microsoft's website. (http://office.microsoft.com/en-us/templates/)

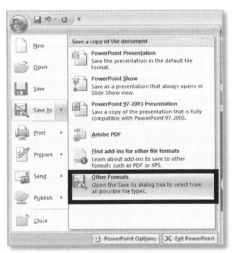

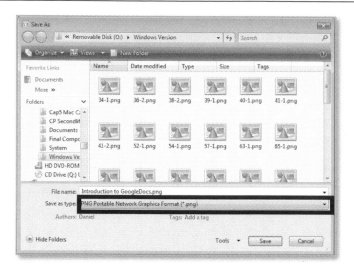

Saving PowerPoint as a Graphic File

You can use PowerPoint to export your template slides into a variety of formats by changing the **Format** option at the bottom of the **Save As** dialog. For Captivate backgrounds, we recommend using PNG format. PNG files are small and show crisp text.

However, not all PowerPoint templates look fantastic when they are exported to a graphics file. If the slide text comes in fuzzy or jagged as a PNG, try saving as a JPG, then a GIF, then a BMP. One of these will work with your font/template combination.

After clicking Save, PowerPoint will ask you if you want to export all of your slides, or just the current one that you are viewing. Make your choice and click OK.

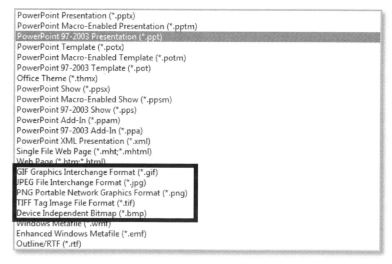

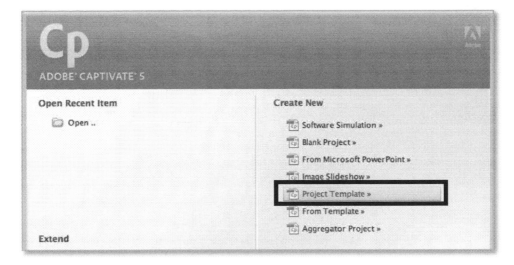

Create New Project Template

Now we're going to create a new **Project Template**. Project Templates are extremely useful in standardizing the look and feel, settings, and components of your projects.

If you are a freelance developer, your general design kit should include several templates of various sizes and styles.

If you work in-house for a company, you should consider using your PowerPoint templates and all appropriate legal markings.

We'll create this project at 800x600, approximately the size of our PowerPoint exports.

 ## PRO-TIP: Preferences and Templates

The project preferences that we told you about in Chapters One and Two will automatically be saved to your new project template. All of your object styles, project settings, and defaults will appear in any future project built on this template.

 ## NEW: Master Slides

Adobe has greatly improved the ability to create Master slides. The functionality of Master slides is similar to the functionality of Master slides in PowerPoint.

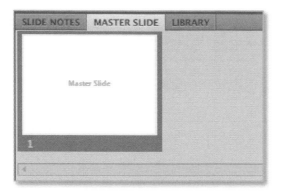

Inserting an Image onto a Master Slide

Once your Project Template opens, you can navigate to your **Master Slide** view by selecting the Master Slide option from the Window menu. When you select one of the slides from this filmstrip, Captivate will display the Master Slide view.

In this example, we are importing an image that we exported from PowerPoint. This image will serve as our master title slide.

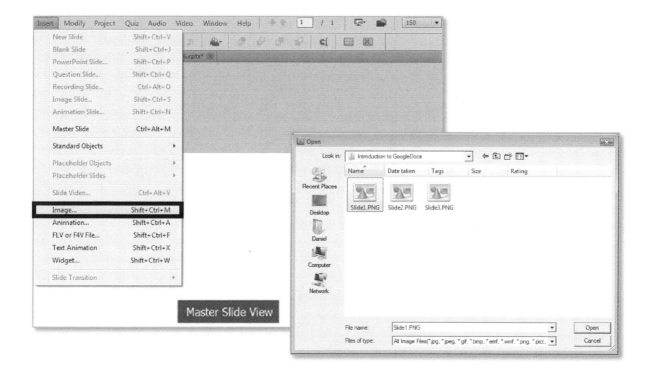

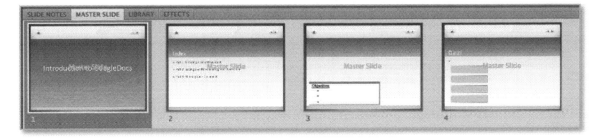

Preparing Reusable Slides

The goal of the process of creating master slide templates is to create as many reusable parts for your future projects as possible. In this example, we've created four basic types of slides: titles, indexes, objective slides, and a quiz.

In addition to the background PowerPoint slides, we've added some basic objects and graphics, like a text caption that will house our objectives in slide 3. (Keep in mind that master slides only support a limited variety of Standard Objects, including text captions, rollover captions, rollover images, and highlight boxes.)

Remember: if you place an object on a master slide, you will not be able to directly edit it from your normal project view. In this case, we cannot edit the 'Objectives' box or the heading of the slide because they live on the master slide. However, we can add transparent text captions in the heading area and next to the bullet points.

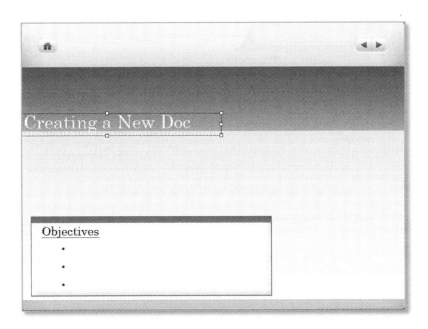

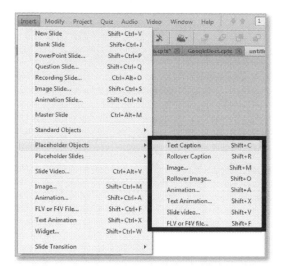

Placeholder Objects

You can create **Placeholder Objects** in your master slides to help you keep your objects lined up from slide to slide. You can see in the screenshot below that we have added placeholder objects for a text caption and an image in addition to the standard text caption that is on the master slide. Placeholder objects will not publish, so you can add them without the end user knowing they're there!

Please note that **Placeholder Object can only be added to a Project Template, not to recorded projects!**

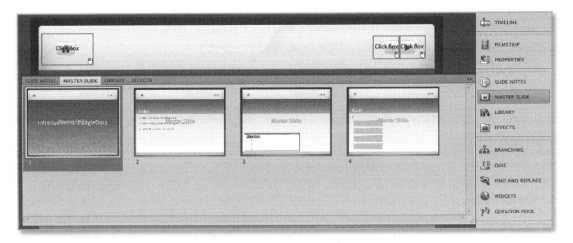

Custom Master Quiz Slides

In this example, we created a nice looking Quiz template slide in PowerPoint, and added it to a master slide in our project template.

Then, we added text boxes and click boxes with success and failure captions to the slide in our new project. This first Quiz slide required a little bit of alignment, but our next quiz slide will be a breeze! We can simply copy and paste the text captions to a new slide that uses our quiz master slide. You will find that this is much faster than creating each slide individually.

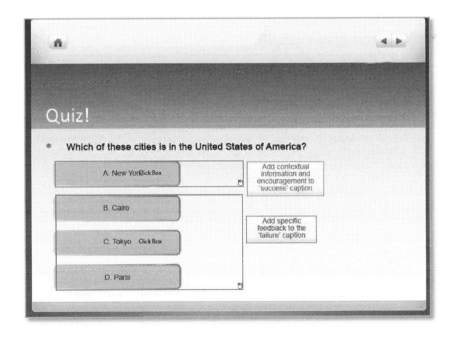

Slide Properties: Labeling and Transitions

You can use the **Label** property in the properties window to name your slides. This is especially useful during the Storyboarding phase of a screen capture project. After you have captured your process, you should label the key parts so you can easily see them later. Not every slide needs a title, but you should definitely label key slides, as well as the first slide in every new activity or section. Labeling slides will also make it easier for you to find the slide in drop down lists and selection menus, such as the Go to Slide__ function.

The slide properties tab also allows you to put transitions into your project. Remember: You should choose subtle, meaningful transitions that don't distract the learner. Transitions take some small amount of time to complete, and every second of a user's attention is valuable in eLearning. The goal is to gain their attention, not to give them a seizure.

For example, a nice **Fade** or **Wipe** between slides can help the user mentally prepare for the next segment. This is similar to using section headings to transition readers from topic to topic in a document.

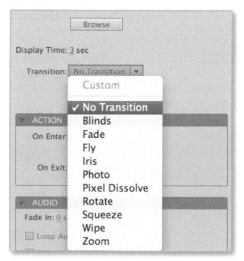

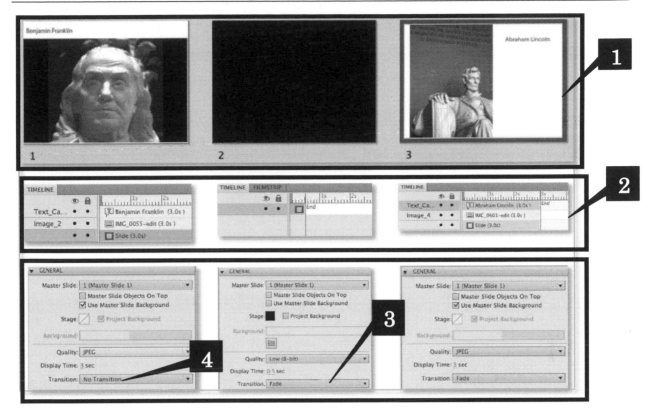

PRO-TIP: Cinematic Effects – Fade to Black

Captivate movies are slide-based, so creating smooth, movie-like fades to black can require a little trickery. We've put together this example to show you how to set up your slides so that they fade smoothly from one scene to another.

1. In the example above, we can see three slides in the Filmstrip: Benjamin Franklin, a plain black slide, and Abraham Lincoln.
2. Old Ben and Honest Abe appear for three seconds each, but the black slide only appears for .5 seconds.
3. Let's look at the General Properties menus for the three slides (3). Specifically, let's examine the **Transition** drop-down. There are several kinds of transitions in this menu, but bear in mind that **transitions are applied to the beginning of a slide, not to the end.** This means that a placing a fade on slide two causes it to fade in from slide one.
4. You can see that Ben Franklin has **No Transition** attached to his slide, while the black slide and Abe Lincoln have their transitions set to **Fade**. This will cause the movie to fade smoothly from Benjamin Franklin to black, then from black to Abe Lincoln.

Creating Slide Groups

If your project has 50 or 60 slides, you should consider using the **Create Group** function to group the slides into manageable units.

1. When you create a group, the Filmstrip will automatically bundle your slides together under into one **Group Slide.** This makes them much easier to drag around. You can also expand groups to see all of the slides inside by pressing the **Expand button** at the top left of each slide group.
2. You can use the properties menu to change the slide group's title, master slide usage, and group color. You can change a whole group's master slide through this menu.

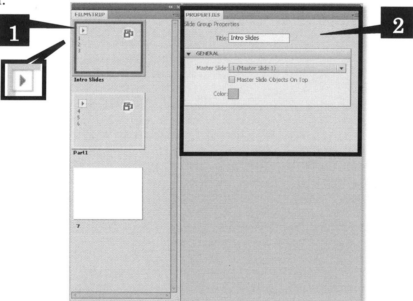

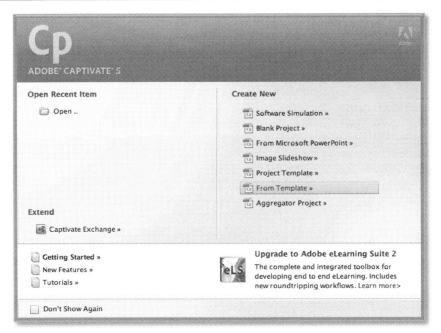

Using the Template

When you save your template, Captivate will create a **.CPTL** file on your hard drive. You can then use the **Create New – From Template** option on the start screen to load your template into a new blank project.

Chapter 9
Quizzes and
Question Slides

In this chapter

This chapter will take you through quiz settings and slides including:

- Setting up Quiz Reporting Preferences

- Understanding Quiz Default Labels Preferences

- Understanding the Quiz Menu

- Setting up Quiz Slides

- Branching Scenarios as Assessments

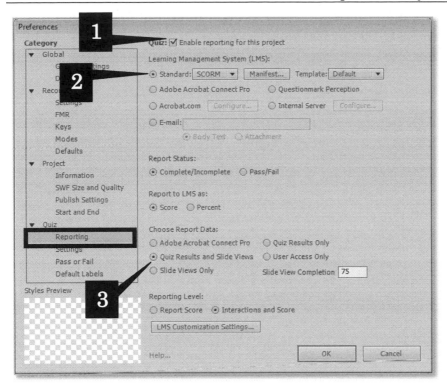

Quiz Reporting Preferences

Now that we're discussing the Quiz and Reporting sections of the options menu, we should note that you will definitely want to contact your LMS administrator, IT person, or vendor before messing with these settings.

If you definitely want to track your learners' progress, you can set the following defaults that might work with your LMS.

1. Check the **Enable reporting for this project** box.
2. Select an option in the **Learning Manage System (LMS) menu.**
3. Under the **Choose Report Data** menu, select **Quiz Results and Slide Views.**

    These settings are fairly generic, and should work for most LMSs. Contact your local LMS guru for help, or check the Adobe Captivate user community on the Adobe website.

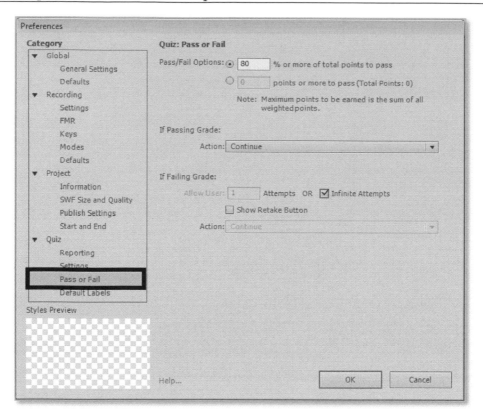

Quiz Pass and Fail Preferences

The **Pass or Fail** menu allows you to change the Pass/Fail requirements for your project. You can choose the percentage of points needed for the learner to pass (**Pass/Fail Options**), as well as what happens if they pass or fail (**If Passing Grade/If Failing Grade**).

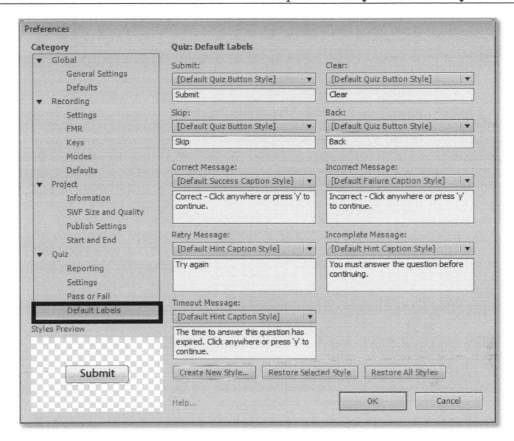

Quiz Default Labels Preferences

The **Default Labels** menu contains the settings for the **Question Buttons Labels** and **Question Feedback** features. These are buttons and feedback that Captivate can automatically generate for your quizzes.

You can leave these settings alone until you have a particular reason to change them.

The Quiz Menu

The **Quiz menu** allows you to create and manage interactive evaluations within your project. To add a quiz slide, you can select the **Question Slide...** menu. This will cause the **Insert Questions** menu to appear.

You can create a variety of quiz types through this menu by checking or unchecking the boxes next to the quiz. You can also specify how many of each slide you want created by changing the value in the input box. See pages 158-165 of the **Captivate User's Guide** to find out more about each type of quiz slide.

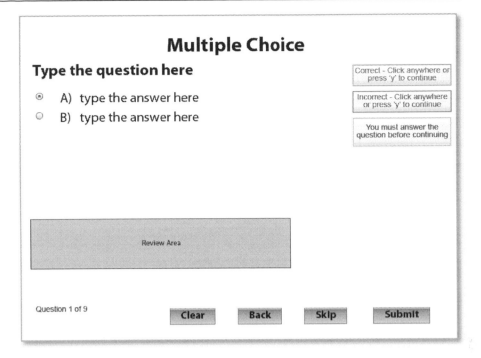

Quiz Slides

Once Captivate creates your Quiz, you'll notice that it's fairly Spartan. You will have to create a background, move the text fields, and configure the properties to make this usable as a final product. This is a lot of work, for relatively little pay-off.

PRO-TIP: Creating Your Own Quizzes

In general, we recommend that you create your own quizzes using click boxes and other objects. The table below describes alternate ways to evaluate the same behaviors using ordinary objects and slides.

(Remember: You can easily create your own quiz backgrounds and templates in PowerPoint. Also, refer to the Objects chapter for more information on click boxes and text-entry fields)

Also, be sure to include some kind of feedback for each success and failure box. Feedback is the most valuable part of these exercises, as they give the students an opportunity to find out why they were right or wrong. Studies also show that learners tend to remember wrong answers more clearly than right answers, except where clear feedback is included.

Quiz Type	Objects Needed	Description
Multiple Choice	Click boxes	Write question and answers in text captions. Then place click boxes (with success and failure captions) over top of the captions. You can change the text captions and reuse these slides.
True/False	Click boxes	Place success/fail click boxes over text captions.
Fill-in-the-Blank	Text-entry fields	Use text entry fields and add the correct answers into the answers field.
Short Answer	Text-entry fields	Create an open-ended text-entry field by unchecking the **Validate User Input** option in the Properties menu.
Matching	Text-entry fields	Add the corresponding correct answer to the text-entry field's answer field.
Hot Spot	Click box	Place a click box over the hot spot. Check **Show Hand Cursor Over Hit Area** to make it easier for your learner to identify the correct area.
Sequence	Text-entry fields	Place correct answers into text entry fields, and have users type correct number of image/step into field.

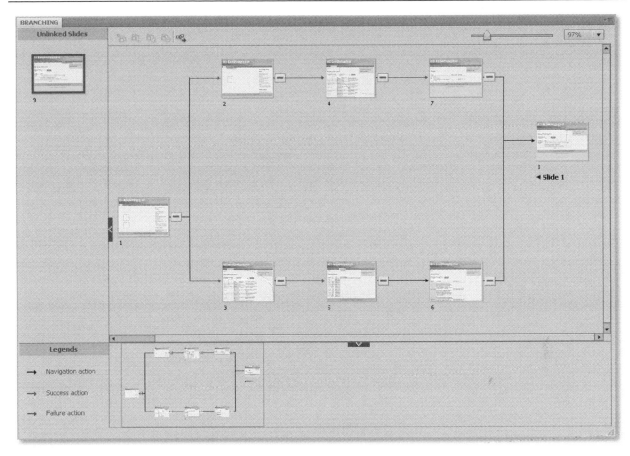

Branching Scenarios as Assessments

Let's imagine that you needed to develop training for a complicated procedure that requires your learners to use their own judgment. For example, you might need to teach users how to proceed through a complicated product return process, or a new conflict management technique. Linear eLearning lessons can tell the learner what to do, but they are not necessarily effective at developing independent thinking.

As we noted earlier in the book, you can use branching techniques to create decision-based scenarios for users. You can use click boxes and the Jump to Slide actions to carefully map these pathways. In this example, we have a project that diverges based on which click box a user clicks on the first slide. The user then proceeds through three slides (2,4,7 or 3,5,6), and ends up at a shared closing slide (8). You'll also notice that slide 9 is in the **Unlinked Slides** category because no slide links to or from it.

If you turn on the Reporting feature for your branching click boxes, you can track and evaluate how your learners performed during their scenario. Try to calculate the minimum number of decision points that a user must successfully navigate, and set your Pass/Fail options to that value.

You can also export this view of your branch pattern as an image using the **Export Branching View** option.

Chapter 10
Pre-Publishing

In this chapter

This chapter will help you get ready to publish including:

- Previewing Your Project
- Spellchecking Your Project
- Using Find and Replace
- Setting up Round-Tripping and Importing the Round-Trip Doc
- Localizing Your Content
- Resizing Your Project
- Increasing the Project Area
- Cropping Your Project
- Sending for Shared Review
- Setting up the Skin Editor
- Creating a Table of Contents

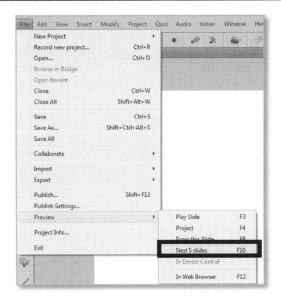

Previewing Your Project

Now that you have captures, objects, audio, and video in your project, it's important to see how they all look together. You can use the **File | Preview** menu to see what your slide animations will look like to the end user. You should use the various Preview options throughout the development process, but more frequently as you get closer to the end of your project.

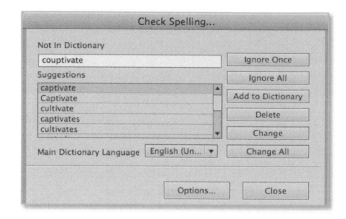

Spellchecking Your Project

You can use the **Project | Check Spelling (F7)** option to check the spelling of all of your documents, captions, and slide notes, much like Microsoft Word. You should always do this before submitting a prototype for review.

Find and Replace

You might find that a key phrase, product name, or piece of jargon has changed since you started your project. You can use the **Find and Replace window** (available from the Window menu, or by pressing **Ctrl-F**) to search for and replace these terms throughout your project.

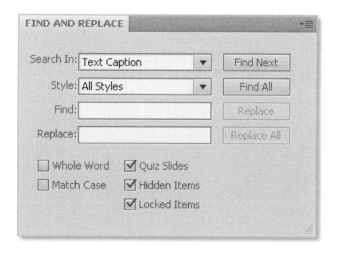

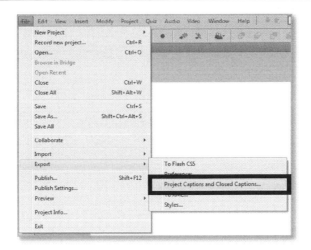

Round-Tripping

At this point in the pre-publishing process, you should focus your efforts on polishing your project. You'll want to make sure that all of your closed captions, text boxes, and transparent shape-captions all have correct content and spelling. This is actually a daunting task if your project has 60 slides, each with closed captions and text objects.

Fear not! This is a perfect occasion for you to **Round Trip** your project to Word using the **File | Export | Project Captions and Closed Captions** option. Round-Tripping your project to Word sends all of your captions and text-carrying objects to a Word document. These are the only text-carrying objects that the end user will see, so you will want to make sure that your spelling and formatting are consistent.

DO NOT change anything in this document but the **Updated Text Caption Data** column! Captivate needs the rest of the information to remain intact. Also, do not change any of the objects in your project until you import your changes back to Captivate.

Adobe Captivate		Sunday, July 18, 2010			
Slide Id	Item Id	Original Text Caption Data	Updated Text Caption Data	Slide	
908	926	Type success text here	Type success text here	1	
908	928	Type failure text here	Type failure text here	1	
908	930	Type hint text here	Type hint text here	1	
941	955	This is an answer square.	This is an answer square.	2	
941	974	**This is a question square.**	**This is a question square.**	2	
941	975	Text caption 1 text	Text caption 1 text	2	
941	999	Text caption 2 text	Text caption 2 text	2	
941	1017	Text caption 3 text	Text caption 3 text	2	

Slide Id	Item Id	Original Text Caption Data	Updated Text Caption Data	Slide
908	926	Type success text here	Type success text here	1
908	928	Type failure text here	Type failure text here	1
908	930	Type hint text here	Type hint text here	1
941	955	This is an answer square.	This is an answer square.	2
941	974	**This is a question square.**	□□□□□□□□	2
941	975	Text caption 1 text	Text caption 1 text	2

Importing the Round-Trip Doc

After you have made your changes to the Word doc, save the document with a new name (1). Then, return to Captivate and use the **File | Import | Project Captions and Closed Captions** (2). This will automatically import your captions back to their respective slides.

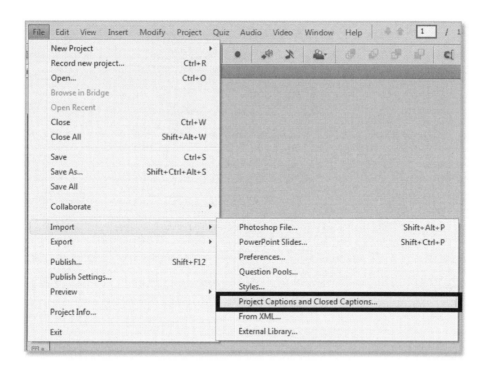

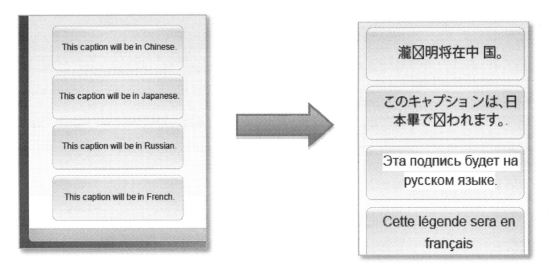

Localizing Your Content

You can use Captivate and **Google Translate (http://translate.google.com)** to customize your lesson text for multiple cultural and linguistic audiences. Captivate accepts Unicode text. This means that we can copy translated text from Google **(1)** and paste it into our Word Round-Trip file **(2)**.

Don't worry if you see boxes in place of the non-English characters in Word. Captivate will show the characters properly when you import the changes (most of the time).

Note: Google Translate is not a substitute for a professional translator. However, if you cannot afford a translator, Translate can help you get to a point where a native speaker can smooth out the rough edges of the translation.

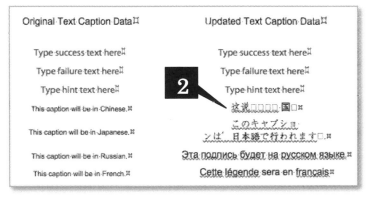

Resizing Your Project

The **Rescale Project** menu contains a number of powerful tools that you can use to adjust your project's size. In essence, you can use this menu to make your project bigger or smaller. More importantly, you can customize the ways that this rescale occurs through the **If new size is larger** and **If new size is smaller** options.

 ## PRO-TIP: Use Caution When Rescaling

The Rescale Project menu is useful for many things, but it is an irreversible process. We recommend that you change your project's size using HTML, after you have published the project. We'll take you through this process in Chapter 10. **Do not use this menu to rescale your project.**

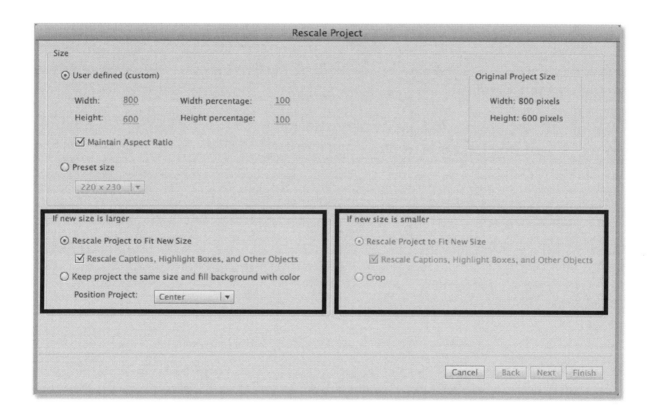

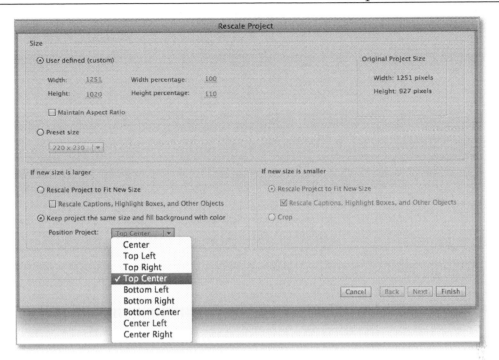

Increasing the Project Area

If you want to add a custom navigation area to the bottom of the project but you don't have the room, you can use the rescale menu to add more space to the bottom of the project.

First, uncheck the **Maintain Aspect Ratio** box and increase your project's height by 10%. Then, select **Keep project the same size and fill background with color.** Finally, choose where you would like Captivate to place your project in relation to this new space. By selecting **Top Center**, Captivate will place your slides above the new space.

Remember: Once you press **Finish**, you can't undo your changes to the project size.

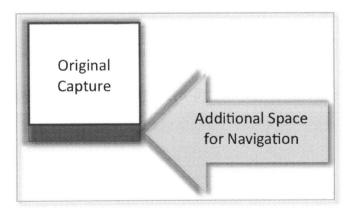

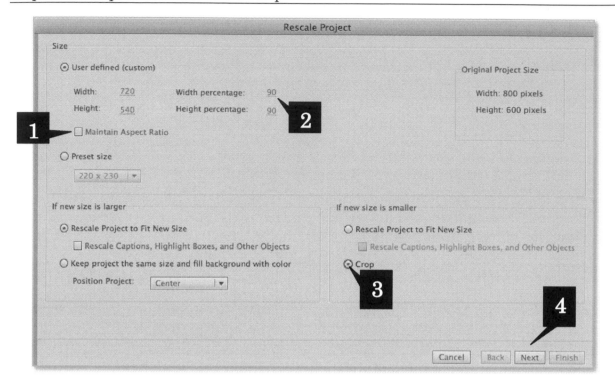

Cropping Your Project

You can also use the Rescale Project menu to quickly **Crop** all of your slides. This is very useful if you captured screenshots in Firefox and now want to remove the browser bar from all of your slides (as we discussed in an earlier chapter). To access the Crop menu,

1. Uncheck the **Maintain Aspect Ratio** box
2. Reduce the height or width in the width
3. Select **Crop** from the **If new size is smaller** menu
4. Click the **Next** button to advance to the **Select Crop Position** screen.

Selecting the Crop Position

You can move the green boundary around to select the area that you want to crop. If your box is too large, or not large enough, you can use the **Back** button to return to the previous screen. Continue tweaking the Width and Height of the project until your box fits perfectly over the content that you want to include.

Once you have the box in sized properly and positioned over your captures, use the **Apply to All Slides** button to make this the default position for the crop. You should then advance through the slides using the arrow buttons.

As you go from slide to slide, you'll find that you can manually change each individual slide's cropping. This is great if you want to move the crop box to include the browser bar in one slide where you enter a web address, but crop it out in another where the bar is not used.

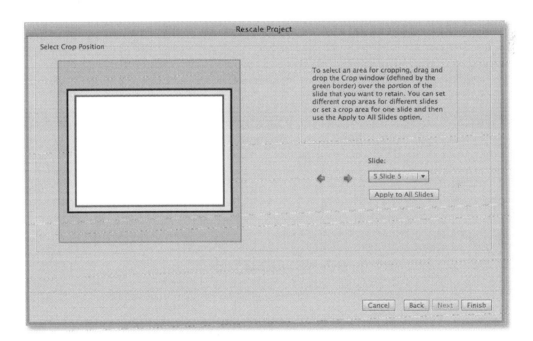

PRO-TIP: Cropping Website Screen Shots

Some websites and programs display the user's name at the top-right corner of the screen. We recommend that you crop that area out, if possible.

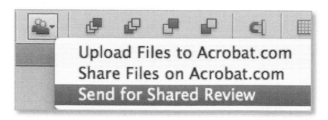

Sending for Shared Review

If you're feeling adventurous, you can try the **Send for Shared Review** option in the upper left of the screen to create a **Captivate Reviewer (.crev)** file. This file allows your clients and SMEs to comment directly on your movie and send these comments back to you. You can then review these comments in the Captivate interface.

All of your clients must install the **Adobe Captivate Reviewer** application to make use of this process, and that can be hard to accomplish. The Captivate Reviewer application is written in a programming language called Adobe AIR, and runs well on both Mac and PC. The software is easy to install, and it's quite fun to use.

People are lazy about installing the Reviewer AIR application, but don't be discouraged. Gently nudge your reviewers to install the software. If that doesn't work, offer to install it for them and teach them how to use it.

When you see the **Send for Shared Review** screen, choose an output location. You might want to consider publishing it to a common server, if your workplace has one.

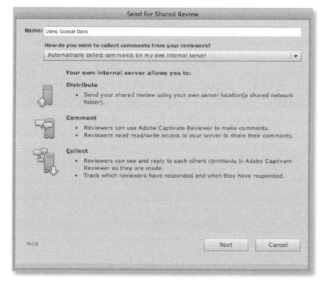

We recommend checking the **SendMail** box, and clicking the **Attach Review (.CREV file)** and **Attach Adobe Captivate Reviewer** boxes. You can click the **Email** button to proceed to the next screen.

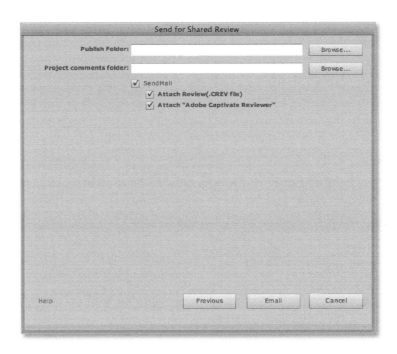

On this screen, you can enter a To: address, subject, and message. When you click the send button, Captivate will send your reviewer a copy of the Captivate Reviewer (.CREV) file, as well as the Captivate Reviewer AIR application.

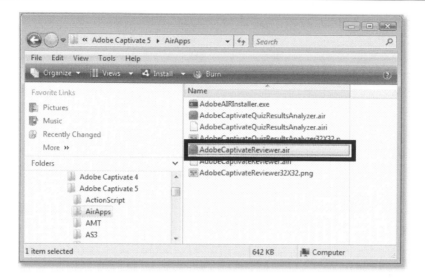

Installing the Captivate Reviewer

Let's take a look at how to install and use the Captivate Reviewer so that you can see how to install it on your clients' computers.

You can double click on the **AdobeCaptivateReviewer.air** file in your Captivate directory to install the Reviewer application.

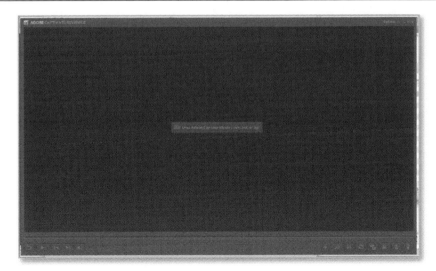

Loading and Annotating a Project

When the Reviewer appears, it will ask you to enter a name and email address. This information is used for tracking changes and will be stored with the .CREV file.

You can click the **Load Captivate Movie** button and select your .CREV file from your computer. You can add comments to the video by pressing the **Add Comment** button in the toolbar.

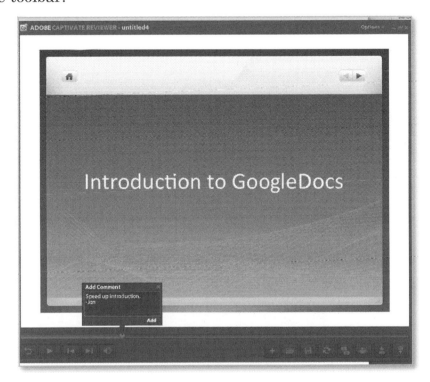

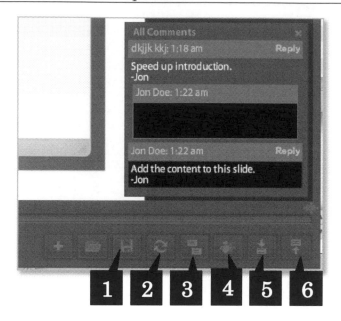

Saving Revision Notes

You can use the Revision Notes tools at the bottom right of the Captivate Reviewer to manage your review files. You can use the toolbar to

1. Save the .CREV file
2. Refresh the comments from a shared network directory
3. View all of the comments and responses in the project at once.
4. Import XML comment files from other users
5. Export your comments as a .XML file
6. Import your comments to Captivate using the **File | Import | From XML** option

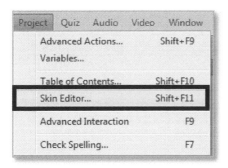

The Skin Editor

Before you cross into the Publishing phase of your project, you should open the **Skin Editor...** and make a few changes to your **Project Skin**. The skin includes the **Playbar** buttons. In this screen, you can set the skin, the published **Playbar** position **(1)**, layout **(2)**, buttons **(3)**, and colors (4).

We recommend customizing your project skin based on the kinds of colors that appear in your captures and title slides. If you choose to include the playbar in your published version, you'll want to create a cohesive color scheme that complements your captures and is easy to see. Also, consider some of the 508 principles that we've discussed throughout the book.

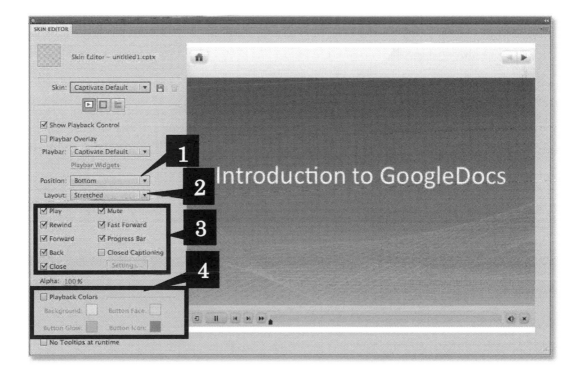

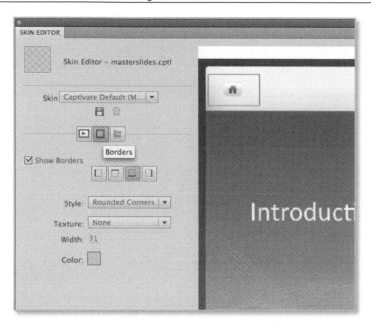

The Borders Menu

You can also access the **Borders** menu from the Skin Editor. The Borders menu allows you to choose how your movie sits within the HTML frame that Captivate generates when you publish your project. Let's look at some of the menu options. You can:

1. Uncheck the **Show Borders** option to turn borders off
2. Select the sides of the project that will have borders
3. Change the style of the borders, and their texture
4. Increase or decrease the border width
5. Change the color of the background HTML

 PRO-TIP: Turning off borders

Borders can cause your project to expand beyond the viewable area of a browser window, requiring your users to scroll to see parts of the movie. You might want to consider turning them off if your project's capture size is already very large. Also, Captivate may create an additional .SWF file in your published output if you leave Show Border checked.

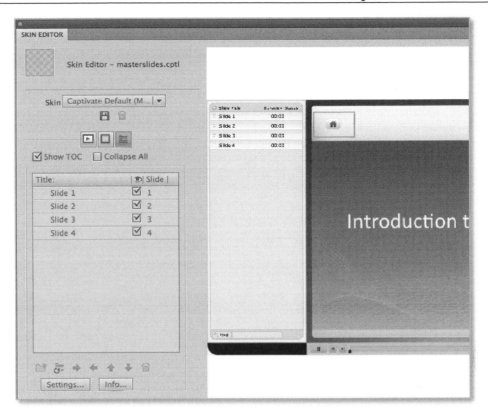

Creating a Table of Contents

The **Table of Contents (TOC)** menu allows you to create a convenient table of contents for your users. You can turn on the TOC by checking the **Show TOC** box in the menu. In the order window, you can uncheck slides to remove them from the TOC, or move them up .

You can also open the **TOC Settings** menu to control the styles, positions, colors, sizing, and font settings for the TOC. You can use this to customize the look and feel of your table of contents.

Also, you can use the **TOC Info** menu to add details to your table of contents, such as the project name or author.

Chapter 11
Publishing Your Project

In this chapter

This chapter will provide you with the information you will need to publish projects including:

- Setting project publish settings

- Using the Publish menu

- Publishing to PDFs, self-contained files (.exe), and documents in Microsoft Word

- Using the Aggregator

- Resizing the Project through HTML

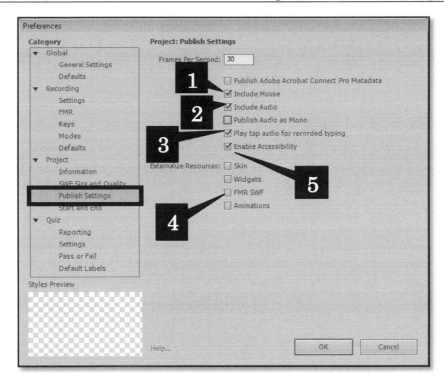

Project Publish Setting Preferences

The **Publish Settings** menu has a number of useful options, but we mostly leave them alone. Here are a few of the options that you might want to know about:

1. **Include Mouse.** Unchecking this box will turn the mouse off in the final published video.
2. **Include Audio.** Unchecking this box will turn off the sound when the video is published.
3. **Play Tap Audio**. When you type text into a field while recording a movie, Captivate automatically adds a 'tap' sound during playback. This sound is good for drawing attention to the typing, but it can get in the way of your voiceover. Unchecking this box will turn off the tap sound in the final video.
4. Uncheck **Externalize Resources – FMR SWF**. Externalizing your FMR files will reduce your file size and loading times, but this can cause problems over some networks. We recommend disabling this option unless your users are in a low-bandwidth environment.

508 Accessibility TIP: Enabling Accessibility

You must check the Enable Accessibility checkbox for the Accessibility setting in the project to take effect. **(5)**

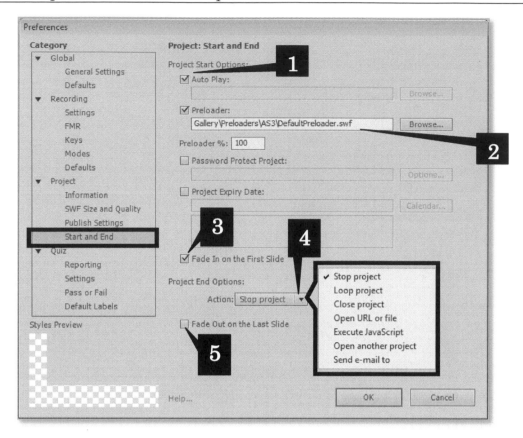

Project Start and End Preferences

We recommend the following settings on this menu:

1. Check **Auto Play** to ensure that your project starts as soon as it buffers.
2. Select a **Preloader** from the **Adobe Captivate 5.0/Gallery/Preloaders**. We like **DefaultPreloader.swf**
3. Check **Fade in on the First Slide** for a nice fade-in effect.
4. Select a **Project End Options – Action.** We like our projects **to Stop Project** on our final slides, but you can also refer users to another page, such as an index or an assessment.
5. Uncheck **Fade Out on the Last Slide**. This animation can confuse users when they reach the end of the project.

PRO-TIP: Using a Preloader for PDFs

If you plan to use your SWF as an animation embedded in a PDF document, use a still image as the Preloader. The PDF will show the still image, which is repeated on the first slide with a click box so the user can start the animation. If the PDF is printed out, the still image will be on the page.

The Publish Menu

Once your publishing settings are set, you can click the **Publish** button at the top left of the screen to open the **Publish menu**. You can use this menu to output your Captivate project into a variety of formats.

The **Flash (SWF)** menu allows you to output your file for web browsers. You should take note of a few key options here:

1. The **Title Field**. The field in this text will appear in the browser title area.
2. You can use **Publish to Folder** to create a new folder for your project. This is good if you're tracking versions, but sometimes you just want to drop your files into an existing directory.
3. Under the **Output Options**, you can check or uncheck the **Export to HTML** option to prevent Captivate from overwriting any custom html or JavaScript that you may have saved to your index file.

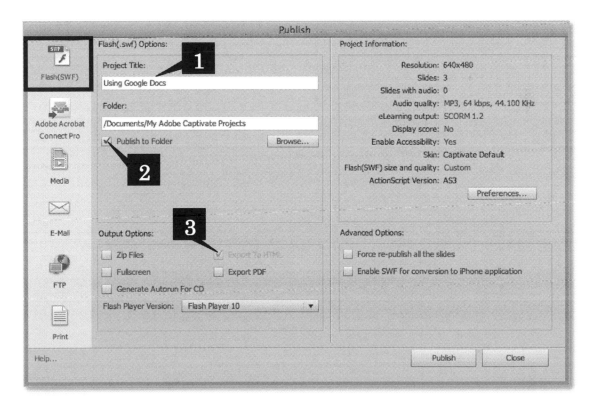

Publishing as a PDF

You can also check the **Export PDF** button to simultaneously export a version of your movie that is contained within a PDF document. Adobe Acrobat is one of the mostly widely installed cross-platform programs on the planet, so this is ideal if you have a mixed Mac and PC audience. PDF files are also easy to email, as most anti-virus systems ignore them. You can also create interactive pages that you can merge or insert into text documents in Adobe Acrobat Pro.

Instructional designers are continually experimenting with the synthesis of text, still screenshots, and instructional movies. These tools provide more possibilities than ever.

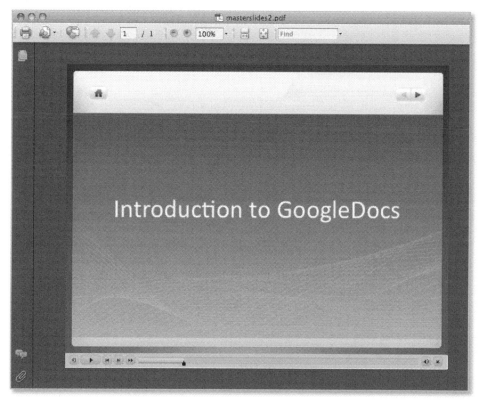

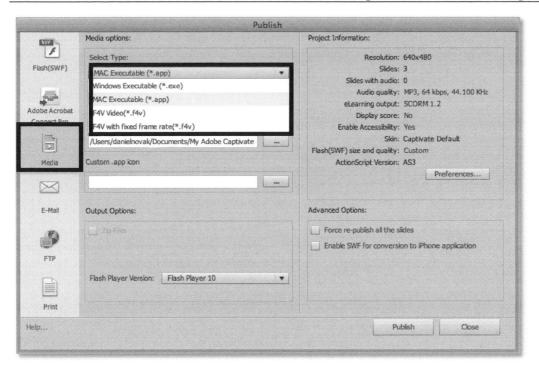

Publishing Self-Contained Files

You use the **Media** menu to publish your Captivate as self-contained executables for both Mac and PC, as well as in F4V video format (without interactivity).

This is useful if you want to create a custom performance support tool for your clients. For example, if you are training seasonal call-center employees, you could use Captivate to create a branching decision-tree application to guide them through a customer refund call. The employee could download it from your server and run it directly on their desktop.

PRO-TIP: Publishing PDF files vs. exe Files

Check with your IT department before publishing any .exe files. Aside from their normal use, .exe files can sometimes contain viruses. As such, some anti-virus systems go berserk when they see .exe files as email attachments, and some systems won't let you email .exes at all! You might have to burn your .exe project to a disc.

If you want to create a self-contained file that you can email, try publishing your project as a PDF.

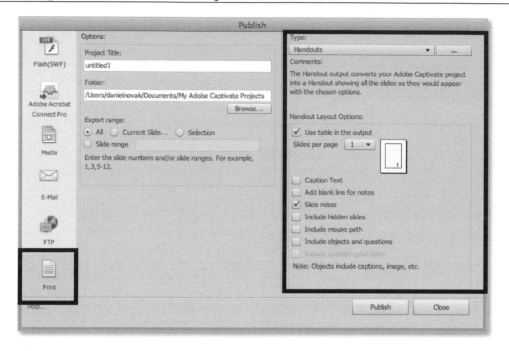

Publishing as a Print Document

You can also publish your slides as a Microsoft Word document through the **Print** menu. This is exceptionally useful as a storyboarding and review tool. If you check the **Handouts Type** and check the **Slide Notes** box, Captivate will output a document with screenshots and your script. You can then use Word to save the file as a PDF, which you can easily email to others.

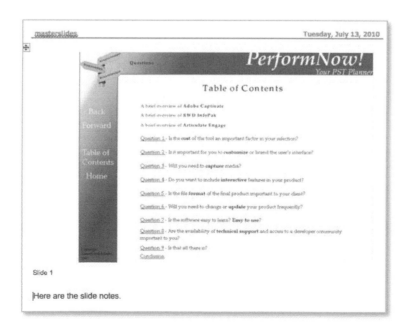

The Project Aggregator

You can use the **Project Aggregator** to combine several of your published SWF files into one Captivate Project. This is really useful if you have several modules that need to be delivered to user all at once.

You can add projects to the Aggregator using the plus sign below the table of contents. You can also use the up and down arrows to rearrange the file order. You'll notice that this file order is reflected in the automatically generated Table of Contents.

You can use the **Publish** button at the top of the Aggregator to open the **Aggregator Publish** menu. Here, you can choose the export format, title, and Publish Options for the aggregated project. Note that you can choose to export it as an HTML file or a PDF.

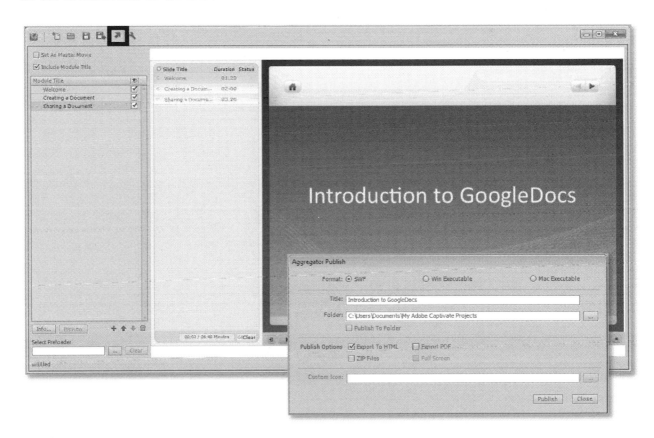

Name	Date modified	Type	Size
standard.js	2/16/2010 4:03 AM	JScript Script File	10 KB
Welcome.htm	7/31/2010 12:59 AM	Firefox Document	2 KB
Welcome.swf	7/31/2010 12:59 AM	Flash Movie	288 KB

Resizing the Project through HTML

When Captivate publishes your movie for the web, it creates three basic files.
1. **x.htm** – The html frame that will keep display your Captivate movie
2. **x.swf** – The flash movie file of your project
3. **standard.js** – A fairly simple JavaScript file that we can ignore for the moment.

In an earlier lesson, we told you not to bother resizing your project using the Rescale Project menu. That's because we can rescale this project through the .htm file without changing your .CPTX file! This process is much easier than it looks, so let's calmly and carefully walk through the process.

One of the goals of our publishing process is to create a movie that fits completely into a user's browser area without scrollbars. Users have diverse technological circumstances, so you will need to assume a lowest common denominator for their desktop sizes, and publish your project at a size that will fit their desktop.

In general, we assume (and http://browsersize.googlelabs.com supports) that most users have their desktop resolutions set to at least **1024x768**. However, many new computers have higher-resolution desktops that are closer to **1280x1024**. If you display a file made for 1024x768 on a 1280x1024 desktop, it will look very small and the user might find it hard to see.

In this section, we're going to show you how to use HTML to resize your project, and automatically present the user with the correct size movie for their computer. Let's take a look at a brief summary of the process, and then proceed in more depth. And the end of this process, you should have a website that automatically detects a user's desktop size and smoothly redirects users to a Captivate movie that fits their desktop and browser.

Summary of Resizing Process

1. Publish your project
2. Make two copies of the **x.htm** file and rename them: **index.htm, big.htm,** and **small.htm**, for a total of three .htm files.
3. Insert the upcoming Javascript into the **index.htm** file between the **<head></head>** tags.
4. Use the **Rescale Project** menu to find two sizes that will fit your project (one that fits within a browser at 1024x768, and one that fits in a browser at 1280x1024)
5. Plug the corresponding numbers into the **SWFObject Width and Height** fields in big.htm and small.htm

```
<!-- Copyright [2008] Adobe Systems Incorporated.  All rights
reserved --> <!-- saved from url=(0013)about:internet --> <!DOCTYPE
HTML PUBLIC "-//W3C//DTD HTML 4.01 Transitional//EN"
"http://www.w3.org/TR/html4/loose.dtd"> <html> <head> <meta http-
equiv="Content-Type" content="text/html; charset=utf-8">
<title>Welcome</title> <script src="standard.js"
type="text/javascript"></script> </head>            <body
<bgcolor="#ffffff"> <center>             <div
id="CaptivateContent">          </div>
<script type="text/javascript">      var so = new
SWFObject("Welcome.swf", "Captivate", "801", "632", "9", "#CCCCCC");
```

Your .htm file

After Captivate publishes your files, you can open the .htm file in your favorite text editor. Let's take a look at some of the most important parts of the .htm file that Captivate publishes. **Do not change anything except the following variables**:

1. The **Head** tags. These mark the start and end of your file headers.
2. The **Title** tags. Anything you enter between those tags will appear at the top of the internet browser. You can change this to a module number, a lesson title, or anything else.
3. The **bgcolor** tags. This value (displayed in hex) sets the background color for your html page. Try to find a color that compliments your movie or toolbar, or enter 'black' to create a cinema-style experience.
4. **SWFname** variable. If you want to reuse this HTML template elsewhere, you can copy this file to a directory that contains another movie and change the SWFname variable to the name of the new SWF.
5. **SWF Width**. The width of your Captivate movie. You can change this to resize the movie without altering your original .cptx file.
6. **SWF Height.** The height of your Captivate movie.
7. **SWF Border sizes**. The border size of the movie.
8. **SWF Border color.** The border color.

We're also going to make two identical copies of the x.htm file that Captivate publishes, and rename them **big.htm** and **small.htm**. We'll also change the x.htm name to **index.htm**, so that users arrive at that page first. Afterwards, your directory should look like the image at right.

Using JavaScript to Redirect

You will need to insert a small piece of JavaScript into the heading of you index.htm page to forward users to the right sized movie for their desktop resolution. Let's take a look at the process of setting up this JavaScript.

1. Open your index.htm in a text editor
2. Navigate to http://www.pageresource.com/jscript/jscreen.htm and copy the JavaScript below

```
<SCRIPT language="JavaScript">
<!--
if ((screen.width>=1280) && (screen.height>=1024))
{
 window.location="highres.htm";
}
else
  {
    window.location="lowres.htm";
}
//-->
</SCRIPT>
```

3. Paste the code between the just before the </head> tag of **index.htm**
4. Change the **screen.width** variable to 1280 and the **screen.height** variable to 1024
5. Change **highres.htm** to **big.htm**
6. Change **lowres.htm** to **small.htm**
7. Save the changes to your index.htm file

For those of you not familiar with JavaScript, this script is basically an *if-then* statement. "If the screen is greater than 1280×1024, go to page x. Otherwise, go to page y."

This chart will help you follow the series of events that occur once the user lands on your index.htm page.

Your index.htm file will now automatically forward users to the correct sized movie for their computer.

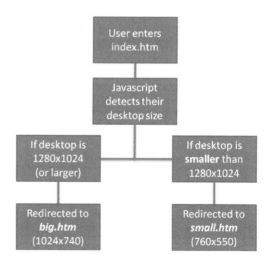

Big.htm and Small.htm Sizes

The table below summarizes a set of project sizes that will fit comfortably into a browser without ruining the aspect ratio of your video. You can create your own custom sizes as needed, but these will fit into a standard browser window:

We recommend starting your initial captures at **1147x830** so that you can use our numbers below. This is a very large capture size, but we will shrink it by changing the SWF Width and Height in our big.htm and small.htm files.

Initial capture (1280x1024 desktop)	**1147x830**
Big.htm (1280x1024)	1024x740
Small.htm (1024x768)	760x550

PRO-TIP: Using the Rescale Project Window as a Calculator

You can use the Rescale Project window to calculate alternate sizes for your project. We recommend using our numbers, as those dimensions fit nicely into a browser window in their respective desktop resolutions. Make sure to keep the **Maintain Aspect Ratio** box checked.

Changing SWFObject Width and Height

Once you have a set of values that works in both resolutions, you'll need to enter them into your big.htm and small.htm files. Let's step through the process:

1. Open big.htm and small.htm in your text editor
2. Find the **SWFObject Height** and **Width**
3. Replace their current values with the values above

If you get it right, the html code should look like this:

Big.htm: SWFObject("Welcome.swf", "Captivate", **"1024", "740"**, "9", "#CCCCCC")

Small.htm: SWFObject("Welcome.swf", "Captivate", **"760", "550"**, "9", "#CCCCCC")

PRO-TIP: Reusing your Files

Now that you have created your index.htm, big.htm, and small.htm, you can reuse them in all of your future projects! Just:

1. Save copies of your modified index.htm, big.htm, and small.htm to a new folder
2. Copy your index.htm, big.htm, and small.htm files to the directory where you have just published a new project
3. Open the big.htm and small.htm files in text editors
4. Change the Title tags to your new title in big.htm and small.htm
5. Change the SWFname in the big.htm and small.htm to the name of the new .swf file (i.e. Welcome1.swf)
6. Save your files.

Finally, uncheck the **Export to HTML** project next time you publish an updated file to that directory. That way, you won't have to worry about extra files floating around. Everything else will work just dandy!

The Final Result

With all of that hard work behind us, your files should seamlessly redirect your users to the appropriate page for their desktop sizing. You can see above that the scale of the 1280x1024 video is considerably greater than the 1024x768.

You can also see why a user on a netbook (resolution: 1024x600) might have a hard time viewing the much larger movie.

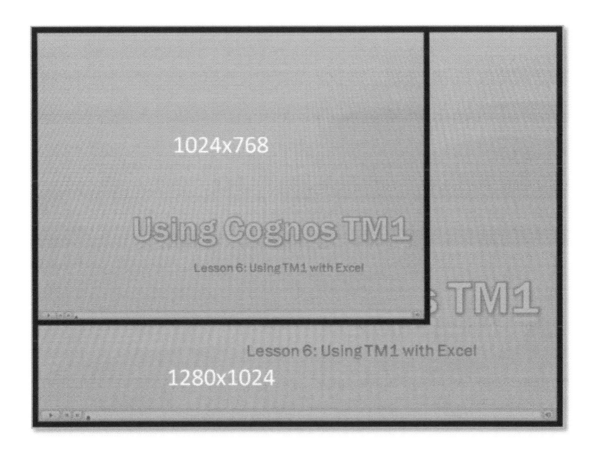

Chapter 12
What's Next?

In this chapter

This chapter will help you improve your products using Adobe Captivate 5 including such suggestions and concepts as:

- Starting small
- Linking into the user community
- Reading blogs
- Watching YouTube

"Secrets" to Improving Your Products

Now that you've built up a degree of familiarity with Captivate, you should start to see that your continued improvement as a developer will be hard work! Your skills will grow best if you surround yourself with skilled developers and designers, seek out opportunities for practice, and keep up with ever-changing technological trends. This may seem daunting, but you will be richly rewarded for your hard work.

Let's close this book with a few ideas about how you can continue to improve your instructional development skills.

- **Start with Small Projects.** Developing and managing large, complex courses in Captivate can take a lot of skill. We recommend that you start small, with simple capture-based projects until you feel more confident. You might even find that simple movies are adequate for most of your needs.

- **Join the Adobe Captivate User Community.** If you have an Adobe ID, you can easily post questions on the Adobe Captivate Forums. If you go to address below, you'll find a whole community of developers who can help answer your questions.

  http://forums.adobe.com/community/adobe_captivate

- **Read Blogs**. There are a lot of Captivate and eLearning blogs out there, and most of them are pretty good. Get started by reading the official Adobe Captivate blogs:

  o http://blogs.adobe.com/captivate/

  o http://www.adobe.com/devnet/captivate/

- **Watch YouTube**. There are dozens of great videos related to Captivate 5 and eLearning on YouTube,. You can also visit our website (http://InstructionalDeveloper.com) for some videos and examples from this book.

- **Develop a Local Professional Community.** If your workplace does not already have an organized learning professional community, you should create one! Bring your company's trainers, SMEs, and developers together for brown bag lunch discussions, guest lecturers from local university faculty, or collaborative work sessions. The more vibrant your local community, the better you will grow as a designer and developer.

- **Hold Local SIGs**. If you can, try inviting people from other companies or schools into your learning community for a **Special Interest Group (SIG)**. Invite people to give a presentation on their current work, recently discovered process, or a book review. This can help provide infusions of new ideas into your organization.

- **Go to National eLearning Conferences**. If you can afford the trip, check out the Adobe Developer conferences around the country. These are great places to meet developers and get new ideas.

- **Hire a Consultant to Bring in New Ideas**. Last but not least, you can always hire a consultant to bring you new ideas. If you choose the right consultants, you can get valuable feedback on your products.

Please visit our website for information about Consultant Services including:

- o **Project review**
- o **Custom onsite training seminars**
- o **Custom webinars**

Email us at: ConsultantServices@InstuctionalDeveloper.com

Index

Index

Thank you for choosing *Rapid Development with Adobe Captivate 5 for Windows*. We worked very hard on this book, and we are always looking for ways to improve its utility. Please send questions, comments, and critiques to Daniel@InstructionalDeveloper.com

Please visit our website at http://InstructionalDeveloper.com for free videos, sample projects, other books, and information about our affordable webinars and consulting sessions.